Islam is polluted and confused by the acts of the lunatic fringe, Ramadan and Eid are times when Muslims show that theirs is a religion of engagement, charity, thoughtfulness, and conviviality. **Scott Korb** only had to travel as far as New York City's East Village to find this out (**page 125**). **Joseph Azam** went all the way to Afghanistan (**page 58**).

I like the idea of holidays being a break from routine. In the case of Christmas, it's a break from our normal, selfish, chaotic lives, a chance to be kinder and more generous; to give gifts, donate what we can to charity, and cook way beyond our ability for people we love. Read about my colleague **Peter Meehan's** lifelong battle to keep his kitchen aspirations in check, on **page 22**; or **Anthony Bourdain**'s fictional account of (and very real advice for) averting bedlam at the dinner table, on **page 164**.

I like Christmas because I like the smell of baking. (I'm monumentally bad at it, but **Dorie Greenspan** makes me want to be better on **page 98**.) I like that it's a time for grand gestures, like constructing *elaborate houses made out of cookies* (**page 46**). I like that you can celebrate Christmas however you want, with whatever food you want, and it's still Christmas. **Michael Snyder** does it Indian style on **page 134**.

But as big of a fan as I am of Christmas, believe it or not, I was not the one w... d... Da... capitalist that he is, suggested we lean into the seasonal mania and surrender to the fact that at this time of year people want turkey and cookies and warm cider, and they want it now. Admittedly, our holiday issue skews a little red and green. But hopefully it'll also reveal some new things about holidays you had no idea about. It did for us.

In any case, whatever it is you celebrate, celebrate it well.

—CHRISTMAS YING

THIS ISSUE'S MENU

PHOTOGRAPH BY MAREN CARUSO

The LUCKY PEACH ATLAS

THIS EDITION: Mike Sheerin is a friend of Lucky Peach and one of our nation's most respected meat cooks. Ask anybody who's ever shared a kitchen with him—he was the sous chef of wd~50 for years, and then ran Blackbird for Paul Kahan—and they will attest to his supernatural talents at dispatching the flesh of ungulates, cloven-toed and otherwise. He's also a hardworking cook, in touch with the need to eat after most people have already gone to bed, so we tapped him for tips on late-night supping in Chicago.

Jim's Original

1250 S. Union Avenue, Chicago, IL

Jim's is just off the expressway, off of Roosevelt, where Jew Town used to be, where the Maxwell Street Market was. Let's just say, for you non-Chicagoans, it's not the best part of town. There are always plenty of bums and hookers floating around. I only go there when I'm drunk and stupid, but you can go early in the night as well, to lay a foundation for the trouble ahead. It's also a good girlfriend barometer: if you can take her here and she likes it, she's a keeper.

Jim's is an old-school Chicago hot dog stand. They do burgers and a great Polish. I think it's the original home of the Polish, and there's really not a better one around.

[Ed. note: In Chicago a "Polish sausage" or a "Polish" is a very distant relative of the kielbasa family—much more like a super plump and distinctively spiced hot dog.]

But the real move at Jim's is to get their pork chop sandwich. It's a thin-cut pork chop, still on the bone—zipped through a band saw, dusted, and then deep-fried. It comes on a burger bun smeared with mustard and stacked with pickled peppers and griddled onions.

Am I proud to tell you how many times I've ended a night face-fucking one of these things? No. Is it going to happen again? Yes.

—MIKE SHEERIN

CATEGORY: Late Night
WHAT TO ORDER: Polish sausage, deep-fried pork chop sandwich with griddled onions and pickled peppers

Chicago, Illinois

MingHin Cuisine

2168 S. Archer Avenue, Chicago, IL

I live right by Chinatown, and this is my regular haunt. It's a dim sum place, and it's great for that—they hit the whole spectrum right on the nose. But it's more often a place I end up late at night. They're open until two a.m., and they're doing good food until the last minute; it's not just a deep-fryer death dive we're talking about here.

They've got all the stuff you might want from a Chinese place, but certain dishes are particularly awesome. There's a beef tendon salad with chili oil and peanuts that I never fail to order. But the thing that always brings me back is this pig preparation they call Macau pork belly. They roast the whole cut then wok-fry the skin so it puffs up. They serve it with just chili oil and sugar. It has the succulence of sous vide pork belly, but it's not sous vide. It's just fucking great Chinese technique. I can never get enough of that, no matter the time of day. **—MIKE SHEERIN**

CATEGORY: Late Night
WHAT TO ORDER: Macau pork belly, beef tendon salad

White Palace Grill

1159 S. Canal Street, Chicago, IL

Chicago, Illinois

The White Palace Grill is a classic Chicago version of a great greasy-spoon diner: run by a Greek family, open twenty-four hours, Formica table tops, the whole deal. And they'll make you quite literally anything you want to eat.

The kitchen is two cooks, just fucking banging it out. The orders keep coming. Pancakes, french toast, waffles, a fucking great burger, biscuits and gravy. They'll do a pork chop sandwich, too. Anything you want, they'll make.

As a cook, there is nothing better than getting a seat with a view of the griddle and just watching those guys crush it. That is cooking; that is service. The Chicago diner is a thing of beauty that any professional will enjoy seeing in action. —**MIKE SHEERIN**

CATEGORY: Late Night   **WHAT TO ORDER:** Whatever you feel like, they'll make it

Copenhagen, Denmark

Kebabistan

1. *Nørrebrogade 162, 2200, Copenhagen, Denmark*
2. *Istedgade 105, 1650, Copenhagen, Denmark*
3. *Nordre Frihavnsgade 63, 2100, Copenhagen, Denmark*

I did not arrive in Copenhagen intending to repatriate to the nation of Kebabistan. But sometimes God opens up the pet door when you thought he was opening a window. And by that I mean that on my first and second nights in Copenhagen this summer (I was there for the fourth MAD conference), rather than indulging in a couple quiet hours of flower-eating at Noma, I ended up at Kebabistan.

Kebabistan is a mini-chain: there are three, all more or less equal from what I've gathered. One eats shawarma sandwiches and french fries at Kebabistan. I was told all of this in advance of my first visit by my guides, oversize Asian twins David Chang and Chris Ying. On *their* first night in town, they had gone to the Vesterbro branch a few hours after dinner at Noma. It seems that the lightness of one of René Redzepi's Nordic repasts, plus a few hours of postprandial drinking, had awoken the need for a hot meat sandwich, and

Kebabistan was from whence it came.

The following day, when I arrived in Denmark, there was a get-to-know-each-other barbecue helmed by the talented and hilarious chef Paul Cunningham of Henne Kirkeby Kro. I had weaseled a solo reservation for myself at Noma that night, but Redzepi, in a move remarkable for both its kindness and brutality, took me aside and said, "You don't want to go to Noma and eat by yourself. You should be here with us." There was no way or reason to argue.

Lambs were roasted. Chris Cosentino grilled sweetbreads. Danny Bowien fried chunks of some impeccable local monkfish and dusted them in his Mission Chinese wing spice. Massimo Bottura was going around grating lemon zest over a risotto-like dish he'd improvised. Albert Adrià and Olivier Roellinger snacked approvingly. And yet as the feast came to a close, me and Chang and Ying stood on formality that, because we had eaten during daylight, more food was needed at night. We hired a cab and cheerily told him, "Take us to Kebabistan!" The guy barely hit the gas as he idled down the street, "You know it's around the corner?"

And so, quite literally moments later we were face-to-face with languidly spinning spits of meat and a humorless

Pozoleria San Juan

1523 N. Pulaski Road, Chicago, IL

The Pozoleria is another can't-miss spot that's a little further north than some of my other suggestions. I can't think of anything more welcoming at midnight than pulling up to this place and seeing the green awning lit up, the neon signs beckoning me in through the bars covering all of the windows.

They have tacos and burritos, and they do guac and chips and all that, but as their name suggests, they specialize in pozole. For my money, it's all about the pozole verde, or as I call it, "the green one." It's a beautiful color—vibrant from tomatillos, jalapeños, and poblanos. It comes with a big plate of accessories: avocado, chicharrones, tortillas, onions, radishes, and cabbage. As far as meat goes, they've got practically the whole hog in there. I've found the jowl in one bowl, the ribs in another—as a meat guy, I really like the mix they dish out.

Like a lot of late-night spots of its ilk in Chicago, the Pozoleria is BYOB. Do you really need another drink if you're at the point where you're swimming to the bottom of a late-night bowl of the green one? That's between you and your priest, but I'd hate for you not to be prepared. —**MIKE SHEERIN**

CATEGORY: Late Night   **WHAT TO ORDER:** Pozole verde, aka "the green one"

---

counterman. Ying and Chang told me I'd be having mixed shawarma—the previous evening they had found that the mixed-meat option was superior to a straight lamb or chicken experience, and I am not one to argue against the superiority of comingled flesh—on "Turkish bread," which in the United States we might call a hoagie or a sub roll. They opted for their sandwiches on durum bread, a disk of flatbread that Mr. Kebabistan toasted on a griddle.

I have a pretty severe persecution complex, so I protested that I was getting the shaft, that they were making me eat my shawarma on white bread because I was a white man and hoarding the ethnic-ier flatbread for themselves. Ying and Chang are acclimatized to my racial paranoia, and waved me off: no, man, the Turkish roll is the play, we're just checking this option out. The sandwich professional assembled our dinner, loading the sandwiches up with every bit of shredded and sliced vegetation under the sneeze guard in a style that we call "dragging through the garden" in my ancestral home of Chicago. Mayonnaise went in. We anointed the sandwiches with spoonfuls of a smoky, dried-tomatoey chili sauce that sat out on the counter and... it was a shawarma sandwich.

A good shawarma sandwich! A filling sandwich that pushed us into the red zone of fullness, the territory of terrifying dreams and uneasy sleep, which was what we had bargained for.

But was Kebabistan the *ne plus ultra* of shawarma stands in Copenhagen? This question, the terrible curse of the food nerd, crept into my mind. Sure we were eating half-crappy food late at night, but were we eating the *best* of it?

The next night we had planned to eat at Kødbyens Fiskebar, which is one of my favorite places to eat in the world, with pristine Nordic seafood and great bread and a little hanky-panky fancy stuff to round out the meal. Again the universe did not see fit to grant me my intended meal. Our group was supposed to be six or eight, but had clown-carred up to sixteen or twenty by the time of our reservation. We had to abandon our plans. So we walked and walked, hungry and hungrier, chasing the red Google Maps beacon back to Kebabistan. We passed countless competing operations on the way. And when we arrived, Kebabistan was jammed up, mostly with other MAD symposium attendees.

To maintain my reputation for insufferability and to make sure that our zombie-hungry horde didn't start eating one another while waiting for

the goods, we formed three teams. One would order a dozen sandwiches from Kebabistan. Tony Kim, from Momofuku Noodle Bar in New York, headed east to the next open shawarma stand to order a handful of sandwiches. And Fredrik Berselius (a Swedish chef most recently of Aska in Brooklyn) and I headed the other direction to do the same. (Neither contingent had to walk more than a hundred yards; that's how many shawarma places there are in Copenhagen.)

Then we reassembled and stood outside of Kebabistan, passing around sandwiches, declaiming and arguing and ultimately submitting to a truth I'd resisted: Kebabistan was the best of the lot, hands down.

Get the mixed-meat shawarma on a Turkish roll with everything. Douse it in the spicy stuff from the bowl on the counter. Get the fries. They're totally factory food, and totally supercrisp, and totally superawesome dipped in superthick mayonnaise outside at night in Copenhagen when you've done a terrible job of making plans to eat elsewhere. —**PETER MEEHAN**

CATEGORY: Late Night
WHAT TO ORDER: Mixed shawarma on Turkish bread, with everything; french fries with mayonnaise

SCIENCE TEAM 3°°°

HUGE FOR THE HOLIDAYS

BY
CHRISTINA
AGAPAKIS

On a Sunday that's usually a week or two after "Western" Easter, my parents set up an electric spit to roast a whole lamb in their suburban Massachusetts backyard. We welcome guests to our Greek Orthodox Easter celebration with a kiss on both cheeks; we nibble on *tiropitakia*, little cheese pies made with phyllo dough, and *kokoretsi*, organ meats wrapped in intestines and cooked on the spit next to the lamb.

ILLUSTRATIONS BY RAYMOND BIESINGER

When the lamb is ready, we begin the meal by cracking open dyed hard-boiled eggs. Over the next few hours, we eat way too much lamb, *moussaka, dolmades,* and *tzatziki,* finishing off with cookies, cakes, and chocolate bunnies bought at deep discount (cheap Easter sweets are one of the perks of celebrating according to the Julian calendar). Happy, sleepy, and extremely full, we adjourn well before sunset to rest and digest.

This ritual will be recognizable to millions of holiday overindulgers. Most will be too sleepy to wonder what's happening inside their cells and nerves, or which enzymes and hormones control the biochemistry of postprandial sleepiness. But as a biologist, I can't help myself.

That you can eat until you feel like you might burst without *actually* bursting tells us a lot about the physics and physiology of the stomach and the neuroscience of appetite. At maximum capacity, the stomach can hold a gallon of food, about sixty-five times its empty volume. As the stomach stretches to accommodate additional food, it inflates like a balloon, pushing against the other organs in the abdomen and making it increasingly uncomfortable to keep eating. Eventually the stomach will start pushing on the diaphragm, making it difficult to take a deep breath.

Well before you reach that maximum volume, the body begins to take action. The stomach is lined with bundles of nerves that can sense the level of stretching and work with

gastrointestinal and peripheral hormones to signal fullness to the brain. Should you press onward past the first feelings of fullness, the nerve signals get more insistent.

Between "full" and reflexive vomiting—the body's final defensive strategy for overfullness—there is a lot of room for holiday overeating. It's easy to ignore those early signals, convincing ourselves that we've still got room to try a few things we couldn't fit on our plates the first time, and still more room for dessert. And, in fact, the abundance of choice presented by holiday feasts actually enhances our penchant for overeating.

The variety-induced overeating typical of holidays is known as the "smörgåsbord effect," and was first identified in 1956 by the French physiologist Jacques Le Magnen. To study the effects of food flavors on appetite, Le Magnen made tiny feasts for rats. When he fed the rats unlimited amounts of a single type of food, they would eat until they felt full, and then stop. But when he gave the rats a smörgåsbord with four different flavors of rat chow, the rats would eat about three times as much as normal, filling up again on each new flavor.

Humans are like rats in that way: when we're eating one food, we get a little more bored and a little more full with each bite—the "hedonic rating" (basically the empirical enjoyability) of the meal goes down with every mouthful. If you've ever waddled out of a fancy restaurant, overstuffed after eating a tasting menu where many dishes were parceled out in tiny portions over a couple hours, you've experienced the reverse: without that sensory boredom kicking in, you can eat more and more enthusiastically throughout the meal.

This phenomenon was rediscovered in experiments on humans in the 1980s. Researchers served varied four-course dinners in their labs and asked the diners to rate their satisfaction at different points throughout the meal. They found that people would eat up to 44 percent more than when offered only a single dish, and that satisfaction and appetite were renewed by each new flavor.

At a fundamental level, our hunger instincts are controlled by the levels of fats and sugar in our bloodstream, and we eat in order to maintain these nutrients at a stable level. When our blood sugar begins to go down, we start to feel hungry, and hormones tell our brain that it's time to eat again. But while we're eating, both sensory pleasure and stomach stretching happen quickly. How we eat—and especially how we eat during the holidays—is influenced by forces beyond just our metabolism and our stomach capacity, namely our willpower and our senses.

Inevitably, we end up ignoring our bodies' early warnings and overeat during the holidays. But how does this all translate to the inevitable postmeal yawns and shuttering of eyelids?

One oft-cited explanation is the sugar high and subsequent insulin crash phenomena. Consider the Halloween feast: kids gorge themselves on pillowcases full of refined sugar. The sugar rapidly enters the bloodstream through the lining of the stomach. Cells in the pancreas absorb the sugar from the blood and start converting it into energy. The subsequent change in the level of energy activates a cascade of biochemical switches. At the last step in the cascade, specialized vesicles inside the pancreatic cells open to release insulin. The hormone insulin controls how the body's cells and tissues process sugar.

All this happens in a matter of minutes. As the fresh dose of insulin flows through the bloodstream, it tells the muscles and fat cells to absorb the sugar and to start converting it into energy. Hence, sugared-up kids bouncing off the walls. But the sugar high has never been proven in double-blind studies: kids get hyper when they get treats whether they have real sugar

or not. The psychology and rituals of food—like the excitement of trick-or-treating—have a bigger effect than sugar itself.

The sugar crash is likewise disputed. Insulin makes our tissues absorb sugar quickly, but that shouldn't cause blood sugar to dip below normal levels. Let's consider another theory. For the post-Thanksgiving food coma, blame often falls on everybody's favorite celebratory poultry: turkey. High levels of the amino acid tryptophan in turkey are converted into melatonin, the hormone that regulates sleep-wake cycles in the brain. Turkey does have a lot of tryptophan, but so do chicken, fish, cheese, and eggs—tryptophan levels aren't enough to explain how sleepy you feel after overeating at Thanksgiving.

What makes holiday feasts sleep-inducing—Thanksgiving, in particular—is the combination of all of the above. First, you just eat a lot during the holidays. The same nerve bundles in your stomach lining that signal your brain to slow down your gorging also tell the brain to divert more of your body's energy to digestion. Second, you

eat a lot of carbs in the form of mashed potatoes, stuffing, and dinner rolls. The simple sugars trigger the release of insulin into the bloodstream. Insulin's main job is to tell cells to absorb that sugar, but it also activates the absorption of some—but not all—amino acids, and raises the relative concentration of tryptophan. Tryptophan gets left behind in the bloodstream; as its relative concentration goes up, more tryptophan can enter the brain, where cells convert tryptophan first into serotonin, a neurotransmitter that makes you feel happy, and then into melatonin, which makes you sleepy.

After all the turkey and stuffing, you may manage to find room for a few bites of pumpkin pie, your appetite reinvigorated by the sight and smell of a new stimulus. The extra dose of simple sugars releases another spike of insulin, and perhaps your brain makes a little bit more melatonin. Sleep is thus irresistible. You pass out on the couch.

In the morning, your stomach is empty or somewhere close to it, your insulin levels are low, and you're ready to do it all over again. ▪

THE DIRTY DISH CLUB
HOLIDAY FOOD DIARY
BY LISA HANAWALT

THE DAYS BEFORE HOLIDAY ARE FOR SIMPLE, FRESH FOODS AND MEALS PREPARED OUT OF MOM'S GARDEN AND DAD'S GARAGE.

1 OVERRIPE BANANA

A PINCH OF STIR-FRIED DIRT

TOFU DOG (MEASURED AND ATE 1 INCH EVERY HOUR)

13 SPOONFULS OF JUICE

3 INEDIBLE LEAVES

SNACKED ON PLUMP CHERRIES

1 BOWL OF CASSEROLE WITH RADISHES + SACRIFICE

HOLIDAY MEATS
TIP: THE HOLIDAY IS A GREAT TIME TO PRACTICE MEAT.

8 SLICES OF HAM, HAT-STYLE

1 BAKED DEEP-SEA ANGLERFISH (DISCARDED THE LANTERN)

6 BUGS →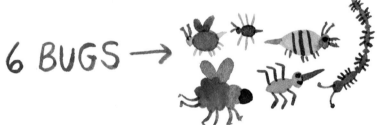

1 COLD CUT CLUSTER

SNACKED ON ORTOLANS (LOST COUNT!)

A BOX OF MEAT

THE HOLIDAY FEAST

ROMAN HOLIDAY

BY **MARK IBOLD** PHOTOGRAPHS BY **GABRIELE STABILE**

When I'm on what the British call holiday, I'm usually crisscrossing whatever foreign city I'm in like crazy, to see this or eat that, to absorb as much as I can in the time that I have. But on a recent visit to Rome, I decided to take the opposite strategy and settle into Trastevere, the neighborhood that Gabriele Stabile, *Lucky Peach*'s Italian photographer, calls home.

Trastevere is just south of the Vatican and across from the central historical district and Testaccio. It's tucked into a bend in the Tiber River, so there's a natural buffer from the busier parts of the city, giving it a cloistered feel despite its central location. The northern edge of Trastevere is touristy, but the farther southwest you wander, the quieter and more residential it gets. I stayed with Gabri and his family just up the hill from the Piazza San Cosimato. Everything was a stone's throw from their apartment: the school, the doctor's office, the train station, even the movie theater (run by the director Nanni Moretti,[1] who pulled up on a Vespa while we were walking by!).

I started my days in Trastevere with coffees at **Bar San Calisto**. As soon as

---

1 Nanni Moretti is an Italian director/film enthusiast/ water polo player. His great films include *The Son's Room* and *Caro Diario*, a portrait of the Italian left that was actually shot in Gabriele's childhood apartment.

I noticed the clientele sitting at little tables outside, I knew I'd chosen a solid morning hang. The average age was probably seventy. One or two people had small scruffy dogs, several were smoking, some were reading the paper. No waiter service. I went into the dark but cheery bar, decorated with old photos of football players, picked a pastry, ordered a coffee, paid the cashier, took the receipt to the barman, got my coffee, went outside, and found a table. Perfect!

I always like checking out the markets and grocery shops when I'm away from home—I get to imagine being a local, and what I'd make for dinner. The Piazza San Cosimato has a small market that's open every day but Sunday with about ten stands. A few sell high-quality produce (not uncommon in Rome); there's a butcher, cheese purveyor, flower shop, and a place that sells household supplies. Right next to the market is a small, fenced playground where children can play while their parents shop.

Just a block away, the **Antica Caciara** is a dream of a Roman grocery. Family-run for over a hundred years, the place exudes good food vibes. *Guanciale* and sausages hang around the doorways; display cases are loaded with top-notch Italian cheeses. The walls are lined with wine bottles, pastas, and dried mushrooms. Wheels of Punturi—a super delicious brand of pecorino Romano better than much of the stuff sold in the States—are piled onto an old cart near the entrance. Turns out that the cheesemaker is the uncle of the guy who owns the shop, and for three generations these two businesses have been intertwined. (Punturi's pastures are in the Agro Pontino, an area near Rome that—according to the counterman—has wetter, tastier grass than the drier Sardinian pastures that are the source of most exported pecorino Romano.)

He explained that the sheep's milk cheese in Rome was commonly called *cacio* until 1923, when the Fascists instituted a law that aimed to create a unified Italian language without dialects, turning *formaggio* into a blanket term for dairy products. But his family kept calling it cacio and called their store Caciara throughout the regime, as a statement of identity.

The term *caciara* also translates to "a mess" in Roman dialect. Back in the 1900s, teenagers from Trastevere were frequently tasked with bringing back wheels of cheese from the countryside. The shops became theaters of action and chaos, due to the large numbers of youth involved. Hence *caciara* also means a messy place, and a raucous, loud situation.

A couple of doors down from Antica Caciara is **I Supplì**, a takeout joint famous for its namesake: fried, stuffed rice balls. *Supplì* can come stuffed with various ingredients, but the ones I had feature a molten-cheese center surrounded by tomato-sauced, plump, chewy, risotto rice, coated in a thin, breadcrumb shell. The whole thing is about the size of a baseball. Supplì are a traditional Roman snack, and are quite popular, judging from the constant line of people waiting to order takeout here. In addition to supplì, I Supplì serves potato croquettes, chicken, and quite good pizza *al taglio* (by the slice).

At the south end of Trastevere, across from the train station, is **Il Maritozzaro**, a little café that specializes in the Roman equivalent of cream-filled doughnuts. *Maritozzi* are glazed, oval-shaped yeast rolls that taste a bit like a simpler version of *panettone*. The filling comes from a bowl sunk into a stainless-steel counter behind the pastry display case. The counterman whips slightly sweetened cream in this bowl (which has a refrigerator under it), then slices the rolls and fills them. After eating two, I ordered another just to watch it prepared—it was made with such skill and ease.

On the way back to Gabri's apartment, I stopped again at Bar San Calisto, where I was somewhat shocked to see the place packed with a younger, arty crowd. I guess it's no surprise that, in a neighborhood that's been inhabited for thousands of years, the old coexists with the new. ◼

VALUES
MATTER

We're hungrier for them than we ever realized.
We want to know where things come from.
We care what happens to them along the way.

We want to trust our sources.
We want to have the information to make meaningful choices
about what we decide to buy and support.
We want people, and animals, and the places
our food comes from to be treated fairly.

The time is ripe.

We are part of a growing consciousness that's bigger than food—
one that champions what's good, and the greater good, too.

Where value is inseparable from values.

WFM.COM/VALUESMATTER

FEAST
of the **ONE**
FISHES

PETER MEEHAN

Photographs by
GABRIELE STABILE

LIKE MANY MEN OF MY GENERATION, I GRATUITOUSLY OVERESTIMATE MY ENDOWMENTS IN MANY PLACES AND PURSUITS,

but nowhere do I so gravely and frequently miscalculate my abilities as when I am in the kitchen. How many times has my wife come home to find me elbow-deep in a pile of ducks with confit on the mind, or been confronted by me barging through the door with hundreds of dollars of Greenmarket bounty and no real plan for what to do with it and no memory that we're leaving town that week? So many times that I'm not allowed to buy ramps anymore.

Is it any real surprise, then, that the first time we decided to stay in New York for Christmas (rather than suffer through the hell on earth that is domestic air travel in December), I endeavored to do a straight-out-of-*Saveur* feast of the seven fishes? A little eel killing, some cuttlefish cookery, a VHS tape of a crackling fire looping in the background? Of course I thought we could do it. That we should do it. That it would be easy and *fun*.

I thought there'd be just a couple friends stranded here for the holidays, that it'd be a challenge to fill the table, that we'd be gathering a sparse few refugees on the Island of Misfit Toys. I couldn't have been more wrong. The list of friends in town with no plans grew and grew, and soon enough, we had just north of twenty people

coming over for a seven-course meal. We owned six chairs. Maybe two dozen plates. There was no way, no how.

I had to face up to the fact that I'd lured in friends with promises of a fancy seafood party that even Delusional Me knew I couldn't pull off.

My wife and I cycled through options. Though I (still) have no idea why it's important that Catholics not eat meat on Christmas Eve, it seemed like a worthwhile restriction to adhere to, if mainly because our pescatarian hairdresser friend was so psyched about it. Bouillabaisse? We'd traveled down that road before—it's fraught with opportunities for error, and I didn't need that pressure. A school of whole fish swam through my mind, as did doing them in some kind of ornate pastry encasement in

homage to Jacques Pépin. It's funny, though, the power of the look in the eyes of a woman who loves you but thinks you're a total fucking moron in the moment. Then, suddenly, it was like, "Lobster rolls?"

At the time, partisan skirmishes were at a fever pitch about the superiority of the sandwiches at Mary's or Pearl (that's Mary's Fish Camp and Pearl Oyster Bar, two Mainer

restaurants in New York). They were a high-ticket item, which lent them curb appeal. And, most important—let's be honest here—they are *easy*. Criminally so. The whole shebang is simple enough to pull off that we did it thirteen days after the birth of our first daughter, and again four years later, when baby number two was just a month old.

That first year, before the kids, before the tradition had become one,

I did some market research: I called a couple people and said, "Hey, you know, we can't do that Italian thing, we're just thinking about doing, like, a Wimpy's-style pile of lobster rolls..."

And with that, our guests multiplied like loaves and fishes. (I'm sure that's not a Christmas parable, but this seems like a safe space to admit to you that I didn't pay a lot of attention in church growing up.) Where once there had been twenty, now there were thirty.

Mark Ibold shucked oysters (years before this magazine enlisted him as its Southeastern Pennsylvania Correspondent), but shucking oysters at a party is for suckers. The next year, he brought what we call the "Fergus Salad"—now I can't imagine the holidays without it. One friend couldn't eat the lobster on account of

wanting to keep her windpipe open and not die, so I made arrangements to make a burger for her. Now, after all the lobster is gone, the griddle turns into burger town, and then those go quick, too. With some chips, some cookies, and some cheese, we stumbled our way into a menu that's become a tradition.

I don't want to count the number of years we've been doing it, for the same reason I try not to notice how much grayer I am every time I look in the mirror. The party has become an established stop for a certain subset of friends (i.e., nonbelievers and those with family in the immediate tri-state area who don't expect them home until Christmas morning). Some bring their in-from-out-of-town family with them; some don't see each other for the other 364 days of the year. There's a lot of catching up to do.

It is not the most ambitious of holiday meals; I think of it as an expensive tuna salad party for friends. But we do it anyway, to bring people together at a time of year when that's a nice thing to do.

THE MENU

Fergus Salad
Lobster Rolls with Potato Chips
Butter Burgers
Cheese (possibly canned)
AK Cookies

FERGUS SALAD,
OR, AS HE CALLS IT, "BEETROOT, RED ONION, RED CABBAGE, CRÈME FRAÎCHE, AND CHERVIL"

Stolen from *Beyond Nose to Tail* by Fergus Henderson and Justin Piers Gellatly

MAKES 6 SERVINGS

Most people know Fergus Henderson as the man who made it okay for rich people in the first world to eat snoots and wobbly bits. Not enough people appreciate the supreme poetry of his recipe writing. We've preserved his instructions as he wrote them because, really, who's gonna do it better? Not us.

The plating of this dish is important: it adds to the pleasure of eating it. Make the red part well ahead of guests arriving or changing into whatever clothes you're going to wear when company arrives.

INGREDIENTS

Healthy splashes extra-virgin olive oil
A little gesture balsamic vinegar
A small handful extra-fine capers
+ sea salt and black pepper
2 raw beets, peeled and finely grated
¼ raw red cabbage with its core cut out, very finely sliced
1 small red onion, peeled, cut in half from top to bottom and finely sliced
6 healthy dollops crème fraîche
2 healthy bunches chervil, picked

A reading from the second book of Fergus:

Mix everything together for the dressing. Toss all your raw red vegetables in the dressing, then on six plates place a bushel of this red mixture. Next to this, nustle your blob of crème fraîche as if the two ingredients were good friends, not on top of each other as if they were lovers. Finally a clump of the chervil rested next to the other ingredients in the friendly fashion. A very striking salad ready for the eater to mess up.

SANTA-STYLE SALAD SACK

Need to bring a dish to a holiday party? This salad is a cinch to throw together à la minute. Show up with your red salad in one bag, chervil in another, crème fraîche in its container, and dressing in an old jam jar (or just dress the salad with what your host has on hand, as Ibold usually does at my place, though we do always confirm beforehand that one of us is in possession of good quality Sicilian salt-packed capers)

ON LOBSTER ROLLS

**K**ingsley Amis wrote a book called *On Drink*, and it is, rather unsurprisingly, one of the finest books on boozing ever committed to felled trees. I bring it up apropos of lobster rolls because there is a chapter where Amis lays out his "Mean Sod's Guide," which is about how to fleece your guests into thinking you're serving them top-shelf hooch when you're not—the dark, cheap side of heavy-drinking hospitality.

Those first lean years, I needed some Mean Sod in my Christmas Eve, some filler in my lobster rolls so that the cost of serving sea-bug flesh didn't sink my gift-buying budget for the year. (Also, I find the purist approach of "lobster plus a little bit of butter in a hot-dog bun" to be the mostest boringest, though I know some Avenging Angel of Coastal Maine will probably strike me down for saying so.)

I selected a recipe for the lobster salad attributed to Jasper White, whose name rings bells for anybody who was into food and out of diapers back when Julia Child was on TV and Chris Schlesinger was a fixture in the national dialogue about American cooking. I liked it because diced cucumber and lobster sounded good together (and they are!), and who doesn't like a chance to throw around a little tarragon?

White encourages the making of mayonnaise, which is not particularly tricky cookery, but who are we kidding? I love the Hellmann's. I subbed Martin's Potato Rolls for the top-sliced buns that are next to impossible to find outside of New England. There is pretty much no food I won't eat in a potato roll—it's the working man's brioche. Hot-dog-style potato buns feel the most generous, the most *soigné*. The twelve-to-a-bag sliced potato roll stretches your dollar the farthest by ratcheting up the bread-to-lobster ratio; it also feels fancier to eat two lobster sandwiches even if it's the same amount of salad as one. Those are what I usually deploy.

Now, bringing this back to where it started: in the early days of these parties, I had more time and the backbone to enjoy hours of tedious labor. So I got my lobsters from a place in Chinatown that sold nothing but lobsters; they'd pack 'em in a heavy-duty corrugated cardboard box that had been used to deliver vegetables to somewhere else, and pad out the box with Chinese newspapers soaked in water. The first couple years, I carried them all the way home. God, those boxes were heavy.

I'd load the tub with lobsters[1] and turn my kitchen into a kill room. The first kitchen that played home to this party was particularly ill-suited to the task, with a single basin sink shallower than a foot bath at a massage parlor. In the early years, I boiled the lobsters. Terrible. Took forever. Steamy, sweaty, hard to anticipate the correct doneness. The house stank of them. Then I switched to steaming in a twenty-quart pot—a gift from one of my first bosses in food—something I had not found a lot of other uses for, but which turned out to be perfect as a death sauna. Steam is not exactly hotter than boiling water, but it cooks like it is and is easier to manage—there's not as significant a recovery time when you add something to the pot, and it's not a wet mess if you wanna pull something out, poke at it, and put it back in. Steaming rules.

Every year, it took a few hours of hatchetry to dismember all the beasts, and at the end, my hands would be pink and delicate from all the incidental pokes and prods of business ends of lobsters and the errant scrapes of shell shards as I fished in the carcasses for more flesh.

And then, one year, things changed. See, I'd been going to Chinatown for the lobsters and then to the Lobster Place in Chelsea Market for supplementary seafood—one year oysters, one year Maine Jonah crab claws, another for shrimp to be cocktailed, etc.—and I always noticed pint containers of just-picked lobster meat sitting there on ice. I am bad at math, but a little scratch work told me that I could go to this place and pay a slight premium for them to do all the killing and picking for me, saving me a full afternoon's work.

And while an assload of lobster shells is a good excuse to make bisque or broth (I like Thomas Keller's tarragon-laced rendition from the *French Laundry Cookbook*, though if you're going to serve more than a thimbleful, you should substitute another liquid for some of the cream, because Jesus, that soup is rich), the trade-off was made, and now it's been a few years since I've done any killing. Assuming that you're buying from a place where they really do their cooking day-of, there's no loss or trade-off in flavor. I haven't looked back since.

Finally, before presenting this package of recipes as the centerpiece of my Christmas Eve tradition, I realized I needed to call up Jasper White to ask him if I could print a version of his recipe, and to find out the origin story of the cucumbers in my lobster salad.

---

1 Sometimes I'd let one roam loose to terrify Oscar, the head case of a Brussels Griffon whom I had the displeasure of owning for a decade, though, to his credit, he usually behaved at these parties.

JASPER WHITE ON LOBSTER ROLLS

"When I started cooking professionally, I learned that cooking in Boston meant cooking lobsters, which was a good reason to learn all about it.

It's shocking to me that lobster rolls have become a national fixation because they're such a quintessential New England dish. It's the way locals eat lobsters—it shows off the qualities of the ingredient while still having a certain humility. New England isn't LA or Dallas; the people with real money drive beat-up Chevrolet trucks and like food they can eat with their hands.

When I had Jasper's, my fine-dining restaurant, I feel like I perfected the bun—a mix of a potato roll and a brioche—and the lobster salad. The salad was originally a mix of celery, onion, lobster, and mayo. I found the celery to be a little harsh—celery is great with crab, which has a more assertive flavor that can stand up to it—and the plain onion could be overpowering. I replaced onion with scallions or chives, and then settled on seeded, diced cucumber to replace the celery. It has crunch and texture but it doesn't get in the way of the lobster flavor.

As far as mayonnaise goes, Hellmann's or Best Foods are perfectly good, but I love a homemade mayo made with grapeseed oil. I don't think it was a very well-known ingredient when I wrote *Lobster at Home*, but I've become a total convert to it since. If you can afford to use it, grapeseed oil gives you a mayonnaise with all the fat and richness you want but lets the flavor of the ingredients in the salad shine through.

At Jasper's, I made my own mayonnaise flavored lightly with tarragon. Nowadays I've moved from tarragon to chervil—they've both got that bright, anise-y flavor, but it's too easy for a cook to add too much tarragon, which can take over. A whisper is beautiful. Chervil is more forgiving; you can't really screw up with it.

A perfect lobster bun should be warm and buttery, with a crisp edge from being cooked on the griddle, and the salad should be cold and pert inside. When you get it right, a lobster roll can be just about the most exquisite thing, even though it's normally served in a paper basket with a bag of chips and a pickle."

LOBSTER-BUYING RULES

The front matter in White's book, Lobster at Home, *about how to shop for and kill lobsters, is worth the cover price alone, and his recipe for brioche-y lobster-roll buns is killer. We've reprinted his rules for purchasing live lobsters here because they are succinct and spot-on and very useful!*

1 **Buy lobsters the day you cook them, and transport and store them carefully.** Make seafood shopping your last stop. If possible, have a cooler ready to store the lobsters in for the trip home. Refrigerate immediately upon returning. Keep lobsters moist, but never on ice. If you cannot avoid an extended moisture shortage, wrap lobsters in a damp sheet of newspaper. Do not store for more than thirty-six hours.

2 **Locate the best source for the most recently caught lobsters.** If you live near the coast of eastern Canada or New England, find a lobsterman or lobster company to supply you with local lobsters. Otherwise, choose the best seafood market in your area. If you do not live in lobster territory, consider purchasing by mail order as a viable option.

3 **Determine the right size of lobster for you.** But remember to be flexible at the market. It is better to buy the best lobsters than to be stubborn about the size you want.

4 **Choose a healthy, lively, freshly caught lobster.** Look at the length of the antennae. If they are short or show signs of algal growth, the lobster has probably been stored in a pound for a long time and may taste bland. Hold the lobster up. If its claws droop, do not buy it. If the lobster shows a frisky disposition by flapping its tail and swinging its claws, buy it.

5 **Always buy the hardest-shelled lobsters you can find.** Give a gentle squeeze to the carapace. Shake the lobster gently. If it "rattles," it may be extremely soft. Check for comparative weight. If the lobster feels heavy compared to a similar-size lobster, it is meaty—an extremely desirable quality.

6 **Never stick your hand into a bag of lobsters.** It is dangerous. Cuts and stabs from lobsters can produce bad infections. A large lobster can crush or rip open your hand or fingers.

7 **Be environmentally responsible.** Never buy shorts (lobsters under one pound), an action that is both illegal and immoral. Avoid canned or frozen meat imported from Canada, where the regulations against using baby lobsters are much less stringent than in our country. Avoid jumbo lobsters over five pounds—let us keep them as breeding stock. If you want a female lobster for a certain dish, check the sex, but do not be greedy. If half your lobsters are female, you will have more than enough roe to go around.

LOBSTER ROLLS

Adapted (and slightly debased) from *Lobster at Home* by Jasper White

MAKES 12 SANDWICHES, SERVES 12

M ultiply as needed. Using burger buns will almost double the number of sandwiches you can get out of this amount of lobster salad, though not the number of people it will feed.

INGREDIENTS

2 lbs fully cooked lobster meat, or the meat from 10 lbs of live lobsters

1½ medium cucumbers, peeled, seeded, and finely diced

1 C mayonnaise

2 t minced tarragon (or **1 T** minced chervil)

6 small scallions, very thinly sliced (or a similar quantity of chives)

+ kosher or sea salt

+ freshly ground black pepper

12 Martin's Long Potato Rolls (aka hot-dog buns) (or **24** Martin's Sliced Potato Rolls)

2 sticks unsalted butter, soft at room temperature

1 If using live lobsters, steam or boil them. Let cool at room temperature. Use a cleaver to crack and remove the meat from the claws, knuckles, and tails. Remove and discard the cartilage from the claws and the intestines from the tails of the cooked meat. (You may also want to pick all the meat from the carcass and add it to the stockpile, or reserve or freeze the carcass for soup or broth.) Cut the meat into ½–inch pieces.

2 Place the diced cucumber in a colander for at least 5 minutes to drain the excess liquid.

3 Combine the lobster, cucumber, mayonnaise, and tarragon (or chervil). If the salad is to be served within the hour, add the scallions (or chives). If not, add them 30 minutes before serving. Season with salt, if needed, and pepper. Cover with plastic wrap and chill for at least 30 minutes before serving, or as far ahead as the night before.

4 When you're ready to party: preheat a griddle over medium-low heat. Taste the lobster salad—does it need more salt? Does it want more mayonnaise? Now's the time to fix it.

5 Lightly butter the insides of the buns. Griddle them for about 2 minutes, until golden brown. (You could toast the buns a little further in a broiler or oven, but that butter-crisped, just-warm interior is the necessary magic.)

6 Stuff the toasted rolls with the chilled lobster salad. Stack 'em high and serve 'em hot.

GRIDDLE BIT OF ADVICE

If you are not a sad little friendless Dilbert, invest in a cast-iron griddle for the house.[1] Get the biggest one your stove will accommodate and watch how many ways there are to use it: pancakes, burgers, bacon, grilled cheese, and more. Practically anytime you're cooking for more than four, there will be a reason to pull it out.

---

[1] Get one even if you are a sad little Dilb, 'cause it'll help you make friends; you're only excused if you're some kinda forward-thinking Kim Dotcom who had a plancha or griddle built in during your last kitchen remodel. I tip my elf half to you, sir.

CHIPSMAS EVE

There is a miraculous synergy between lobster rolls and potato chips that the lazy host or hostess is all but compelled to honor and celebrate. In early years, we had a polyamorous crisp mix going on—some sour cream and onion, some classic, some barbecue, whatever. No fidelity to any one maker or flavor.

Eventually, that grab-bag approach landed a bag of Utz Crab Chips in the mix, which rose above the others like a star of wonder, a star of night, a star with royal burning beauty bright: crab chips were the one and true chip for the party.

I'm not talking some cross-cultural shrimp chip, but potato chips dusted with Old Bay or Old Bay–like seasonings. Herr's is the company that has actual brand-name Old Bay on its chips, so those are worth seeking out, but if Utz's off-brand action is available more easily, I go for that. The artisanal-ish chipmakers of Route 11 have some "Chesapeake Crab" that are worth a spin. If all of these chips sound like they're from Mars to you, you're probably living in a different part of the world and should order crab chips from Amazon. Because, really, that's WJWD.

BUTTER BURGERS

MAKES 8 BURGERS

Butter burgers are a specialty of Solly's Grille, an old spot in Milwaukee, Wisconsin. I first learned of them from *Hamburger America*, a documentary by a mutton-chopped man named George Motz that is among my favorite food films. I first ate a butter burger when Mark Ibold cooked one at my house—he'd seen the movie, too, and gone so far as to seek out the real deal when he was in Wisconsin.

Butter burgers migrated from weekend fare to our Christmas Eve menu the second year we had the party. One for Mark's girl Vicki, who's allergic to lobster, and one for me, who's allergic to not eating hamburgers when I can be.

The following morning, we woke up and made versions of these burgers (I slathered the patties in yellow mustard before griddling them, as In-N-Out does for Animal Style burgers) for Christmas breakfast, which was a tradition we maintained for a few years: burgers for breakfast, sometimes with a half bottle of Billecart-Salmon rosé champagne, a big Chinatown meal as soon as we could eat again, and falling asleep with the sun.

Now they're a fixture of the party, turf to follow the surf. I'm sure the three kings would have done it the same way if they'd made it to Milwaukee before Bethlehem.

INGREDIENTS

1 lb ground beef

2 T kosher salt

+ grapeseed or vegetable oil

8 Martin's Potato Rolls, toasted

+ Hellmann's mayonnaise

a chiffonade iceburg lettuce

1 medium yellow onion,
   sliced into rings

16 crinkle-cut pickles,
   preferably Claussen

16 slices American cheese

1 stick unsalted butter, soft
   at room temperature

+ mustard and ketchup, for serving

1 Ahead of the party: mix the beef with the salt and divide the meat into 16 flattened little patties. Stack 'em between parchment paper in the fridge. (You can do this to order, too, but it's better to get all the meat handling out of the way before party time, in my experience.)

2 Get your griddle good and hot—2–3 minutes over medium-high heat—then slick with a film of oil. Griddle-toast the insides of the buns. (Real talk here: we usually just toaster-oven toast the buns. But griddling the inside is the ideal.) Then condimentize them: spread mayonnaise on the bottom bun and top it with a piece of lettuce, a few onion rings, and a couple pickles.

3 Sear the patties in batches of 4 at a time. After 2 or 3 minutes, they'll be nice and brown and crusty. Flip and top each patty with a slice of cheese. As soon as the cheese has gone gooey, stack 2 patties on top of one another and spatula-transfer from the griddle to their throne of condiments on the dressed buns, which you have ready and waiting. Crown each with a tablespoon of butter and the top of the bun. Serve with ketchup and mustard on hand, and eat hot.

CHEESE

When people ask you what they can bring to your party, even if you tell them they don't need to bring anything, you know what they're gonna bring? Cheese. I don't know why. Life is just like that.

The renaissance of American farmstead cheeseries in the last twenty years has helped ensure your guests are likely to bring something good. If you live in a city like New York and you have high-quality friends, they will suffer through the holiday crowds at Di Palo's, ticket in hand, and get Lou or Sal or one of the family to dish on whichever special cheeses they've got on hand, and you'll end up with that.

But there's a place for less rarefied cheese eating at parties, especially at my parties. Bring me your tired, your weary, your port wine cheeses, and I will eat them.

One year, a handsome scamp named Andrew Knowlton came to Christmas Eve, and he brought a batch of his personal pimento cheese, and the crowds went wild. (Andrew writes for an upstart indie food zine called *Bon Appétit*; he's published the recipe there previously, and I bet you can score it from their real estate on the Internet!)

Another year, our friend Julia brought **blue cheese and gingersnaps**. The cookies were Anna's Ginger Thins, a Swedish-ish supermarket staple; the cheese was maybe a Gorgonzola dolce—any simple but good blue will do. The combination sounds—and maybe is—weird, but it works, especially during the Feliz Navidad time of year, when the collective appetite for spice-spiked things swells like a paunch in an old Christmas sweater.

And then there's the **canned cheese** from the Pacific Northwest, Cougar Gold. Harold McGee wrote about its ageability seven issues ago, so I won't tread too heavily on that path. But I like that it's a cheese you're supposed to age in the can in your fridge. What better way to mark an annual tradition than to give your host a can of cheese and ask him or her to hold onto that for a year until you're back for the next party? They will have a conversation piece to pull out throughout the year, sustenance in the case of disaster, and you'll have subtly marked some territory in their home like a sneaky little terrier.

AK COOKIES

MAKES 24 BIG COOKIES

INGREDIENTS

2 sticks unsalted butter, room temperature
1 C sugar
1 C dark brown sugar
2 eggs
1 t vanilla extract
2 C all-purpose flour
1 t baking soda
1 t salt

1 C shredded unsweetened coconut
1 12-oz bag chocolate chips (or about **1 C** chopped-up chocolate— I use Valrhona)
2 C quick-cooking oats
1 C chopped walnuts or pecans

This is a tough one. And by *tough*, I do not mean difficult, though I will note that I have never made these cookies myself— my wife is an excellent baker, an accomplished maker of all kinds of sweet things that I don't have the skills or attention span to pull off. It's tough in the sense that, for a very long time, this wasn't a recipe for handing out or, even more unthinkable, publishing. It was our secret house cookie—before it, we had been leaning heavily on the Korova cookie (from Pierre Hermé via Dorie Greenspan, which would later become perhaps better known as the World Peace Cookie), which is one of civilization's great cookies—and this recipe became the one we'd only share if you got close enough.

But the truth, evident in their appellation, is that they were someone else's cookie before they were ours. That person is Jeanne Roth, our friend Genevieve's mom. We ate them at her house in Anchorage on a summer day in 2007. My wife remembers falling for the cookies the moment she saw them on the cooling rack, and Jeanne was kind enough to share the recipe. I often have trouble finding clean socks, my checkbook, or my keys, but I know where that scrap of paper is at all times.

They are, without question or hesitation, my ideal cookie. The oatmeal and coconut disappear; there is a melding, a unification, an alchemy where many ingredients become one greater thing. The nuts stay whole enough to add some textural intrigue, the chocolate— which we now hack into helter-skelter chunks instead of relying on the machine drip of chocolate chips—is sometimes a sliver or splinter of joy, sometimes a pooled cocoa-colored lagoon of pleasure. I quite often eat one or more at each meal of the day—they are ideal companions to the first coffee of the day, a buffer between the quiet of dawn and the demands of the day to come. I eat so many, I feel like the moon man waxing toward maximum weight when they are in the house, and the only consolation from the sadness that accompanies their absence is that at least I am not eating cookies all day long. Until she makes them again.

1 Heat the oven to 350°F.

2 Using a mixer fitted with the paddle attachment, cream the butter and sugars on medium-high speed until pale yellow, homogeneous, and smooth. Add the eggs and vanilla extract and mix for another 5 minutes.

Add the dry ingredients in order, mixing them in on low speed, just until each is incorporated into the dough.

3 Use 2 soupspoons or an ice cream scoop to form the dough into lumps about the size of a squash ball. (You can make smaller cookies if you like, or want to feed 'em to kids.)

Scoop all the dough and chill it on a quarter sheet pan in the fridge for at least 30 minutes before baking. If you're not baking the whole batch, freeze the balls on the sheet tray before transferring them into a freezer bag. When you are ready to bake, space them well on a Silpat-lined sheet pan and bake for 11–12

minutes. Let them cool a bit on the sheets, then transfer them to wire racks to fully cool before serving. These cookies are best when they have fully cooled, though you will undoubtedly eat some warm because it will take you years to develop the patience to ignore their siren's call until they are ready. You are only human.

SAINT
JOHN
OF THE
SLIME

JOHN BIRDSALL

ILLUSTRATIONS BY SAM D'ORAZIO

I'M ON A GREYHOUND SOFTLY ROCKING UP THE 101 PAST CLOVERDALE, WHERE THE ROAD BANKS ABOVE SHALLOW GORGES, AND SPINDLY BLACK OAKS PETER OUT SO THE REDWOODS CAN CROWD IN. MY KNIFE KIT'S ON THE SEAT NEXT TO ME AND IN MY DUFFLE, A NOTEBOOK OF SCATTERED RECIPES FROM *JOY OF COOKING*, THINGS I THINK I'LL NEED AND CAN'T REMEMBER: BASIC BATTERS, MUFFINS, WAFFLES (WILL THERE BE A WAFFLE IRON IN A MONASTERY?), A SHEET CAKE. FOR THREE WEEKS, ENDING WITH THE FEAST OF SAINT JOHN THE BAPTIST—A HOLIDAY I'VE NEVER HEARD OF AND, HONESTLY, DON'T EVEN KNOW HOW TO CELEBRATE—I'LL BE 130 MILES NORTH OF SAN FRANCISCO, COOKING FOR A SAINT IN EXILE.

Chef at the restaurant where I cook gave me leave of absence, a "dispensation," she said with tweaking irony, to let me go cook three meals a day for a bunch of bearded, icon-venerating Catholic monks on a mountain above Ukiah.

"Let me know if Jesus wants to hire you permanently for the cult," she said in front of everybody around the prep table, with a laugh that felt like a jab from her fish-bone tweezers.

Maybe I deserved it—me, a kid who thought that being a priest would be cool, until I got older and realized that the vow of celibacy is a lure for guilty gay Catholic boys to stay in the closet. What was calling me this time to put my life on pause, piss off my boss, and be a fill-in monastery cook for three weeks? To go see whether Dan, my broken little saint, was really okay? I told my chef it was a chance to get some perspective on my life as a cook—I felt like I'd been getting stale and she knew it. I told her I needed something to help me get my edge back, and cooking on a mountain somewhere for the obscurest kind of holiday in the world might give me back my sense of purpose in the kitchen, strip cooking back to the basics, allow me to feed people who weren't paying for it and who would be grateful for my labor and not send back a plate of risotto, because they thought it was wrong.

Dan's not literally a saint, but he's gentle, with an awkwardness that touches you like sincerity, and eyes so trusting they make his big nerd glasses look extra ridiculous. He's not even technically Dan anymore, now that he's a monk at Holy Transfiguration Monastery. He's "Brother Damian." He signed himself that way in blue Bic in his last letter, which is absurd to me, since I know him as just another lost and lonely queer kid.

I met him when he was the young director of a Catholic charity in San Francisco that hooks up volunteers with lonely seniors. I signed up because I felt a pull to do something

good, an irrational burst of altruism, but the senior they assigned me for home visits was a sour old Irish lady who loved Jesus and hated the gays. I'd be in Anne's Tenderloin apartment, where the constant shuttling of roaches on the walls was like a lazy headline crawl across the CNN screen, and she'd hawk up some bile about homosexuals and how they were taking over the city. After a few drop-ins, I quit.

At my exit interview, I told Dan everything. And when I came to the part about Anne's homophobia, and how it offended me, specifically, because I'm gay, I watched a familiar expression flick across his face.

Later, around two a.m., as I slept next to my boyfriend, the phone blasted me awake. Dan wanted to know if I'd meet him tomorrow, to talk— there was something he wanted to tell me. I wasn't surprised. My gaydar is pretty good.

We talked a lot in the weeks after that. I was the only out queer he knew; he wanted to know how I went public, the hundred things you want to know before you take that first step out of the closet. He asked me how it feels to get a boyfriend and fall in love. I took him to the Castro once just to walk and be around gay guys. He looked like a puppy somebody had dropped on a freeway.

Dan was from a suburb, felt from childhood that God had a special mission for him. As a teen he entered a seminary down near Stanford, but

cleaver to every last tie of my Catholic upbringing, all the bullshit and fear, the hypocrisy of my teacher-priests in high school. But did I have another, deeper life I was supposed to be living? Something beyond cooking for rich people? Volunteering to visit lonely seniors was the start of that quest—did it lead me to Dan for a reason?

The bus pulls into the Ukiah Greyhound station, and there, as I hoist my knives and my duffle down the steps, I see a Minotaur-chested monk in a black robe with an even blacker beard standing next to a scarred and faded little pickup.

"Welcome," Father Michael says with a smile, setting my duffle in the truck bed next to battered produce boxes and milk crates packed with cartons. And in the cab, before we leave the parking lot, he grabs the dangle of rosary beads hanging from the rearview and, in a voice so deep it's like he hauled it out of a crypt, says, "Lord Jesus Christ my God, be my companion, guide, and protector during my journey, keep me from all danger, misfortune, and temptation, and by your divine power grant me a peaceful and successful journey and safe arrival."

The truck lurches into first gear.

Brother Damian meets me, and hugs me as Father Michael unloads the truck.

He isn't the troubled Dan I used to face across café tables in San Francisco—there's a calm about him, composure in his eyes, above the patchy, pubic monk's beard, under a fresh-buzzed skull. "I want to show you everything."

The monks had fixed up a cell for me, the nicest, all the way at the end of the hall, the biggest and least dank, a thank-you for coming to cook. They'd dragged an old Barcalounger in there and set it beneath the narrow plywood sleeping loft, with its mattress of dog-bed depth. On a shelf above the bed, an icon of the Virgin Mary with a stretched oval face and extremely

the priest who took Dan's virginity was the same one who told him he should go back home, stop wasting his parents' money and everybody's time. Dan left in despair, felt suicidal at times, and lived the next few years as a true believer whose church, for whatever reason, had frosted him. He volunteered to teach poor kids in Kerala, and later landed at the senior drop-in charity in San Francisco. He was the most genuinely good-hearted person I'd ever known.

Then he stopped calling. Almost a year went by before I got a letter from a place called Holy Transfiguration Monastery, the one in blue pen signed Brother Damian: Dan had entered a small Ukrainian Catholic abbey above Ukiah, eight brothers and an elderly abbot, with a tiny chapel lashed together from redwood boards. "All my doubts, those things that were so hard to think about," he wrote. "Everything is washed clean in the holiness and beauty of this place."

He wanted to see me, said he got permission from the abbot for me to come and cook during the weeks leading up to the Feast of Saint John the Baptist in late June, when they'd have a visiting scholar and extra study. It'd be a hardship for the monks to cook for themselves.

"I know that food is your gift from God," Brother Damian wrote. "It would mean so much to have you share that gift with my brothers and let you experience the peace of this mountain." Is this how God calls you, I thought, with a note on flimsy stationery with pink flowers across the top? I told my chef I wanted to go to the monastery to get my sense of purpose back. But what I hadn't told her was that I had this residual twinge that God might actually want me for the cult. Hearing from Dan brought back this old, haunted feeling that maybe I had a higher calling. Coming out on the week of my twenty-first birthday had been an act of taking a butcher's dolorous eyes. Do monks put images like that above their beds so they won't be tempted to rub one out after vespers? I resolve to make Mary face the wall, that night and every night.

We walk up the mountain to a clearing ringed with tall elders. "How are you doing?" I ask. Dan tells me he's found peace here.

The monks spend hours and hours a day praying alone in their cells. Dan tells me Jesus comes to him like a husband sometimes. "It's… intense," he says, flashing me a look. "Like everything I used to think I'd maybe find with a boyfriend. He comes to me, John." I tell him I think that's great, that I'm so happy for him, even if I can't quite understand it. "Maybe I should make you a wedding cake," I say with a laugh.

"The more time you spend up here," he tells me, "the more you'll understand." That evening is the quietest, blackest night I've ever spent. There's so little ambient noise—no distant traffic, no boyfriend snoring—that all I can hear is the roar of blood in my ears and my own breathing. I start to freak out, then think of Dan in his cell down the hall, on his plywood sleeping platform in the crazy quiet of the forest, taking his glasses off to be completely vulnerable for Jesus, naked.

The next morning my work begins: three squares a day for twelve of us, the eight brothers, Father Boniface (the abbot), the visiting scholar, a handyman, and me.

The church and monks' quarters (they call them "cells"), the latrine—they're rustic and wooden, ramshackle in places, built into a steep mountain flocked with primeval redwoods. But the refectory and kitchen have the fluorescent glare and dingy white laminate of a tract home in a subdivision. Not exactly the quaint farm kitchen I was expecting.

The Holy Transfiguration monks take a strict vow of poverty (not like the priests I grew up with, old Father Kenney, downing bourbon highballs at neighborhood pool parties, first in line to load up on London broil at the buffet). In theory this is amazing. In practice, especially for a cook trained in the NorCal school of ingredient perfection, it's appalling.

Each week, Father Michael drives the battered pickup down the mountain to the Safeway, where the clerks set aside the produce culls and the souring dairy. Heads of leaf lettuce bruised and blackened around their twist-tie cinches, irredeemably limp. Flaccid cucumbers, powdered white in parts with bacteria that looks like rime ice. Cartons of milk you shake and hear the solids thumping against the waxboard walls. Nothing is too far-gone to drag up the mountain and stuff into the kitchen's old Traulsen cooler.

"How do you guys not get sick?" I ask Brother Macarius that first morning—he's showing me how to start the oatmeal, and where all the serving pieces live. He flashes a little-kid smile through a scraggly reddish beard and shrugs. "It's still good."

It dawns on me that this gig isn't so much about cooking as it is a painstaking daily process of produce redemption: trimming, cutting away to get at the still-moist hearts of things, reviving in cold water, restoring faded essences in broths.

That first week I make noodles from scratch and roll them out by hand to make a casserole, using an old institutional can of tuna I find in the pantry; I cover it with a cap of bread crumbs crisped in margarine, speckled with oregano from a bush in the neglected garden behind the refectory. I simulate molasses by making a loose, dark caramel flavored with cloves, for quick breads I make from a rescued case of zucchini, the rotted carcasses meticulously scraped for any flesh I can salvage. I braise battered lettuces in broth made from scraps.

The monks keep a place for me at the long refectory table, next to Brother Damian. He smiles when I take a seat, bumps my knee, and flashes a surreptitious thumbs-up for the mushroom bread pudding, the lentil soup flavored with mint that's jumped the dead garden and gone native. One day he taps my leg with his closed hand, then opens it to reveal an icon on a tiny laminated card: Lawrence of Rome, patron saint of cooks. I keep it in my pocket whenever I work, which is all the time I'm not in my cell sleeping.

The abbot, Father Boniface, is a tiny white-haired Belgian, a garden gnome come to life. As a missionary in the old Belgian Congo, he'd come down with something that took one of his legs. He uses the kitchen as a shortcut between his sleeping cell and the church, and every morning as I prep breakfast, he thumps his prosthetic limb across the floor rapidly, and I catch a flash of brown robe and wiry white beard hairs.

Father Boniface had visited monasteries on Mt. Athos in Greece and modeled the rule on things he found there. That included eating without talking, every day but Sundays and holidays, as one of the brothers read aloud some Gnostic text about the dangers of pride, or attachment to one's brothers, or vanity, or gluttony—basically, meditations on not enjoying yourself, with food I try to make as much about pleasure as I can.

One morning gray-faced Brother Macarius comes back into the kitchen with the platter of zucchini bread I'd just sent in. "Abbot says this is cake, not breakfast." The monks' calendar is a confusing schematic of ordinary days, fast days, and feast days. Feast days are Sundays—the brothers get to talk, they can eat a little more, and there's dessert. Fast days it's just water, a little bread if the brothers want it. Ordinary days the monks get three meals, restrained by rules that seem arbitrary and impenetrable. Father Boniface decrees that the chicken soup I eked out of freezer-burnt carcasses is too luxurious to break a fast, the dumplings I made with butter and skimmed fat too silken.

Another morning I stand contemplating two flats of strawberries that should have ended up in Safeway's dumpster, not Father Michael's truck. They're pink and flabby, like they were boiled, swollen like flesh in the grip of acute thrombosis. Here and there is a still-red, relatively firm lobe: I cut it out, drop it into a bowl. The rest I dump in the compost bucket. My fingers are slimy and starting to itch.

I hear the thump of Father Boniface as he enters the kitchen, walks past me, then stops and comes back to see what I'm doing, peering into the compost bucket.

"You're wasting too many."

I want to explode, tell him he's an idiot, ask him how many other cooks from San Francisco with my training would even put up with this shit, for no money. Instead I keep my cool.

"But father, they're—rotten."

He pivots on his prosthetic, starts moving again to the refectory door. "If you look at it that way," he says, "then *everything* is rotten."

John the Baptist is a strange Bible figure, wild and scratchy, a sort of crazy-man save the date for Jesus. When I was a kid, I watched that Jesus movie, *The Greatest Story Ever Told*, and early on, when a sweaty Charlton Heston as John gets his head chopped off in prison, my mom turned to me and said that's who I was named for. He's my saint. I thought, What a lousy protector to have, a guy who spends all his time admitting that he's nothing. He's the saint of losers, of people who aren't special but figure out their purpose anyway.

Basically, the Feast of John the Baptist is a celebration of a prophet who said, "I'm not the real Messiah—that guy is coming later." Christianity is a religion of perpetual waiting, a cosmology of delayed fulfillment. But while you're waiting, you're expected to carry on the best way you can, dealing with all the shitty things in your life, patiently and with good grace, by

being nice to people and making the most of slimy strawberries.

Everybody thinks cooking is about transformation. If you think about food as chemistry, that's true. But a lot of cooking is about taking things as they are and just leaving them that way. It's about copping to the inexorable forces of the universe—rot, souring, and wilt—and making the most of them. So much of cooking is the opposite of transformation. It's not-change. Acceptance.

Since I met Dan I'd made it my mission to fix him, to make his life okay in the ways I thought mine was. To see him come out, get a boyfriend, whatever. That was really why I came to the mountain, to be the Charlton Heston prophet who'd show Dan that there was a better way once he stopped running away from his true gay self. But being here only shows me all the ways I try to hide from my fears about myself, how I avoid looking my patron saint of failure straight in the eye.

I'm seeing how rotten my own life is, how I'm always striving to be a better cook and always being frustrated because I can never be good enough. Or how tenuous and unsatisfying my relationship with my boyfriend really is, the ways I'm always wanting more from him. Father Boniface is right. If I look at it in a certain way, everything in my life *is* rotten. Nothing is ever perfect enough.

Who were we kidding, Dan and I? In the end, I thought the holiday here on the mountain would be about saving Dan from his own delusions, but the truth is Dan invited me because he thought he could save me. But I'm not ready to be a saint, to give up the things of this world, imperfect though they might be, and stay on the mountain, drinking soured 2 percent, waiting for salvation. My way is still the brotherhood of gay club night at 1015 Folsom, getting drunk and seeking benediction in my boyfriend's eyes, even though I know it will end in a horrible breakup and I'll be bitter and

depressed for weeks. It's my cross to drag around, falling in love with imperfect things. I'm not ready to drop it just yet.

The day after my strawberry epiphany, I cook the feast of Saint John the Patient. The abbot gives Father Michael money to buy some nonrotten foods for the holiday, and I make the most of them. I marinate chickens with California bay leaves and a little artemisia I gather from a south-facing clearing, and roast them. I make bread pudding with fresh milk and cream and flavor the sugar with elder blossoms I gathered the week before. Father Boniface says it is a fitting tribute. I was going to say something about how I thought I'd overcooked the chicken a little bit, and that if I'd had it do over again, I would've cut back on the sugar in the pudding, but I decide to let it be. Maybe it is a fitting tribute after all.

I ask to leave the monastery a few days early—I've had enough, plus I'm exhausted. In my cell, I turn the icon of the Virgin so she is facing out again, and I hug Brother Damian before sliding into the truck; Father Michael drives me down the mountain to the Greyhound station.

On the bus back to San Francisco, a woman with a face so red it looks like it's been scalded is freaking out. She's a few rows behind me. Once the bus gets on the 101 she starts asking if anybody knows if there's a liquor store in Cloverdale—our first stop—where she can get a beer and get back to her seat before we pull out again.

She's telling some guy that she doesn't need it, it's just that she couldn't sleep last night and kind of wants something to help her relax. Everybody knows she's lying. "Hey man," she says, out of her seat now and in the aisle next to me. "You know any place in Cloverdale?" I shake my head, give her a smile I hope she takes as empathy, and think her suffering face is the most beautifully human thing imaginable. **LP**

the ●●
Artisän ●●

now playing at
wusthofedge.com

Chef Clayton Chapman
The Grey Plume, Omaha, NE

200 Years of knives   Made in Germany
Solingen

WÜSTHOF
defining the Edge

MIAMI ICING

ARTIST'S RENDERING BY SCOTT TEPLIN

South Beach, 1984. Powdered sugar is king. Money is rolling in like the rising tide. Everybody wants a piece, and those who have it, flaunt it. Every week, gaudy Tuscan-style estates and Spanish villas spring up along Collins Boulevard, on Star Island and Hibiscus Island, in Indian Creek. Each new mansion tests the limits of architecture and good taste. Build a pool, and your neighbor builds a pool on his roof. He buys a tiger, you buy a hippo.

Be careful, though. The fuzz is always watching. And at Christmastime, the department is under pressure to make their quotas for the year. Those who think they're bigger than the system will be made into examples. Fail to pay off the right people, and you just might find yourself caught in the hungry jaws of justice. —CHRIS YING

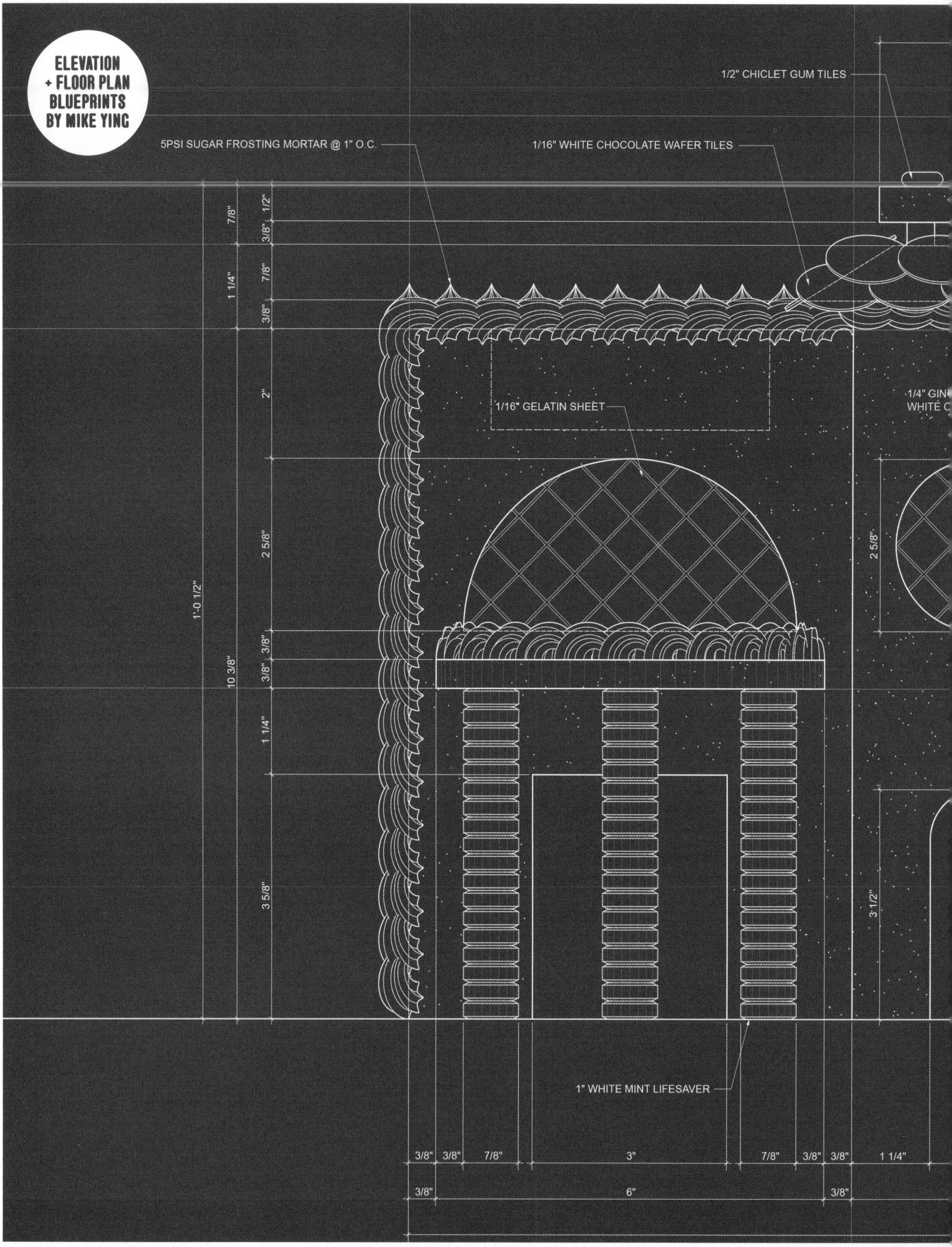

1/2" CHICLET GUM TILES

5PSI SUGAR FROSTING MORTAR @ 1" O.C.

1/16" WHITE CHOCOLATE WAFER TILES

7/8"

1/2"

3/8"

1 1/4"

7/8"

3/8"

2"

1/16" GELATIN SHEET

1/4" GIN
WHITE C

2 5/8"

2 5/8"

1'-0 1/2"

3/8"

3/8"

10 3/8"

3/8"

1 1/4"

3 1/2"

3 5/8"

1" WHITE MINT LIFESAVER

3/8" 3/8" 7/8" 3" 7/8" 3/8" 3/8" 1 1/4"

3/8" 6" 3/8"

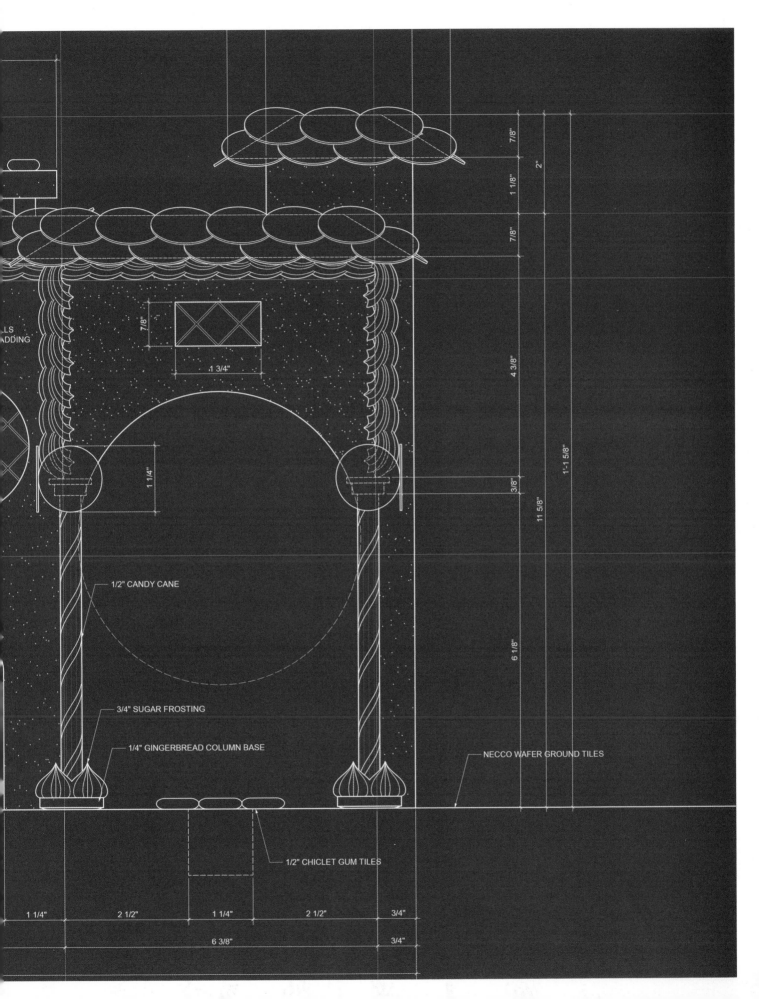

7/8"

2"

1 1/8"

7/8"

LS
DDING

7/8"

4 3/8"

1 3/4"

1-1 5/8"

1 1/4"

3/8"

11 5/8"

1/2" CANDY CANE

6 1/8"

3/4" SUGAR FROSTING

1/4" GINGERBREAD COLUMN BASE

NECCO WAFER GROUND TILES

1/2" CHICLET GUM TILES

1 1/4"   2 1/2"   1 1/4"   2 1/2"   3/4"

6 3/8"   3/4"

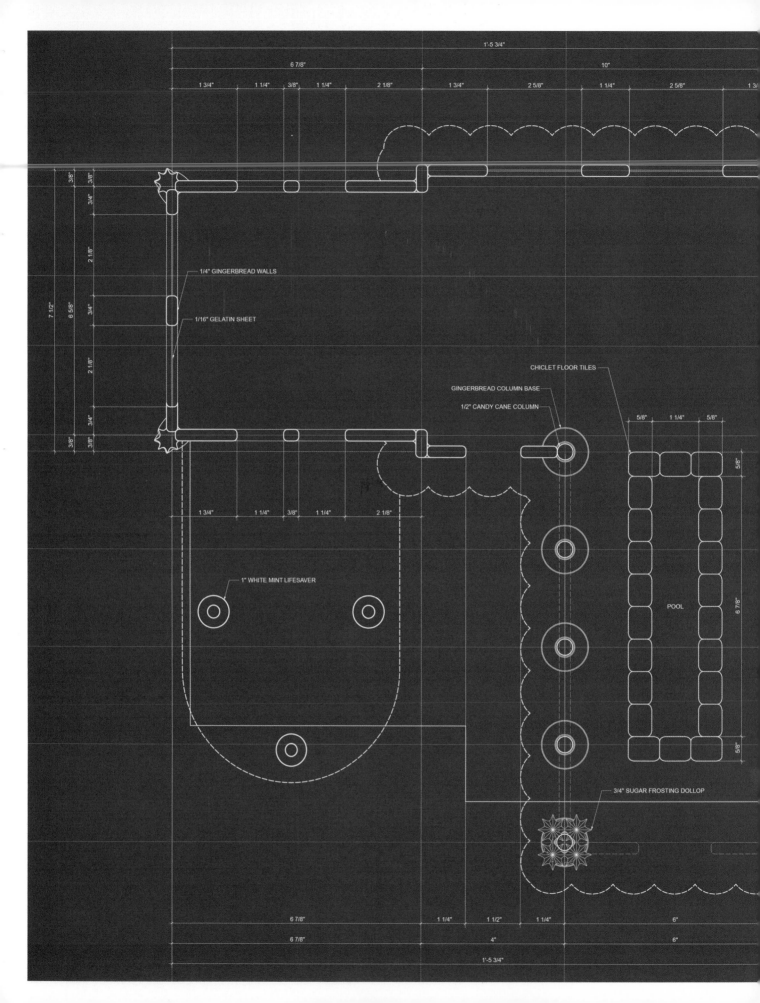

1'-5 3/4"

6 7/8"

10"

1 3/4"   1 1/4"   3/8"   1 1/4"   2 1/8"   1 3/4"   2 5/8"   1 1/4"   2 5/8"   1 3/

3/8"   3/8"

3/4"

2 1/8"

1/4" GINGERBREAD WALLS

7 1/2"   6 5/8"   3/4"

1/16" GELATIN SHEET

CHICLET FLOOR TILES

2 1/8"

GINGERBREAD COLUMN BASE

1/2" CANDY CANE COLUMN

3/4"

5/8"   1 1/4"   5/8"

3/8"   3/8"

5/8"

1 3/4"   1 1/4"   3/8"   1 1/4"   2 1/8"

1" WHITE MINT LIFESAVER

6 7/8"

POOL

5/8"

3/4" SUGAR FROSTING DOLLOP

6 7/8"   1 1/4"   1 1/2"   1 1/4"   6"

6 7/8"   4"   6"

1'-5 3/4"

GINGERBREAD

Makes 1 gingerbread house

½ C + 2 T (175 g)	buttermilk
6 T (85 g)	unsalted butter
1 C (220 g)	light brown sugar
¼ C (85 g)	molasses
1	large egg
5 ½ C (650 g)	all-purpose flour
1 t (4 g)	baking soda
1 t (2 g)	ground ginger
1 t (2 g)	ground cinnamon
½ t (2 g)	fine sea salt

1 Combine the buttermilk and butter in a medium-sized saucepan and gently heat just until the butter is melted.

2 Remove from heat and transfer to the bowl of an electric stand mixer fitted with a paddle attachment. Add the brown sugar and molasses followed by the egg, mixing until thoroughly combined.

3 Sift the flour with the baking soda, ginger, cinnamon, and salt; gradually add the dry ingredients to the mixer bowl, mixing until completely incorporated.

4 Form the finished dough into a flat rectangle, wrap in plastic film, and chill for 1–2 hours.

5 Roll and cut the chilled dough as necessary and transfer to a parchment- or Silpat-lined sheet pan. Bake in a 300 ˚F oven until thoroughly baked, approximately 15–20 minutes (baking times will vary based on the size of the cut dough forms).

6 Remove from the oven and cool completely before assembling your house.

ROYAL ICING

3	large egg whites
¼ t (1 g)	cream of tartar
4 ½ C (450 g)	confectioners' sugar

1 Place the egg whites in the bowl of an electric stand mixer fitted with a whisk attachment. Beat the egg whites on medium speed until frothy; add the cream of tartar, then gradually add the confectioners' sugar, and mix until glossy. It should be thick, with no lumps.

2 Keep the finished icing well wrapped to avoid drying. Use the icing as needed as an adhesive to join the gingerbread forms; alternately, use the icing as a decorative element (dilute with a few drops of water if piping).

Process photographs and recipes by Michael Laiskonis

BAKING +
CONSTRUCTION
BY MICHAEL
LAISKONIS

PHOTOGRAPHS BY
DAVIDE LUCIANO

MAKE THE WORLD YOUR OYSTER WITH PLYMOUTH GIN

Crafted in an English port with a strong maritime heritage, Plymouth Gin is uniquely a product of its terroir, much in the way that an oyster's merroir expresses the characteristics of the area where the bivalve was cultivated. So celebrate the holidays with a most festive pairing: fresh oysters and a Plymouth martini.

DISCOVER OUR TRADITION RESPONSIBLY.

PLYMOUTH® Gin. Product of England. 41.2% Alc./Vol. (82.4 Proof). Distilled From Grain. ©2014 Imported by Pernod Ricard USA, Purchase, NY

PHOTOGRAPHS BY JOSEPH AZAM

HOME FOR THE HOLIDAYS

JOSEPH AZAM

I nervously clutched the worn-out armrests of my seat through the harrowing approach into Kabul International Airport. The jarring welcome felt only appropriate, given how long it had taken me to make this first trip back to Afghanistan.

The small contingent of diplomats and other mostly American VIPs on my flight were met on the tarmac and whisked away by heavily armored black SUVs. Military and paramilitary passengers filtered out into secure areas of the parking lot and into their own small convoys. The rest of us walked to a dimly lit terminal where our passports were processed in a proud display of the country's revitalized bureaucracy that allowed for more than a few minutes of reflection: nearly three decades after being smuggled out as a parcel under my mother's arm, and just in time for one of the most important holidays in the Islamic calendar, I had found my way back to the place that I had known only through borrowed memories.

It was January 2006. Crestfallen and exhausted after my first round of law school exams, I was desperate for an escape that would restore some texture to what had quickly become a one-dimensional existence. I wanted to reset in a space as far away as possible from my life in San Francisco. It was a period of relative calm in Afghanistan. In the weeks prior to my trip, relatives in Kabul told me that the International Security Assistance Force (ISAF) and diplomatic convoys had been responsible for most of the deaths in the city as they sped through the streets, refusing to yield to pedestrians. As long as I looked both ways before crossing, I would probably be fine.

Choosing to travel to Afghanistan in the dead of winter, however, was a rookie mistake. Kabul was covered in a miasmic winter blanket—a frigid mix of dust, exhaust, and gasoline fumes that burned the eyes. The noise pollution was equally unforgiving: horn blasts from military convoys, pulsating helicopter rotors overhead, and the constant drone of gas-powered generators. None of it, however, could take away from how remarkable it felt to be in my birthplace, really, for the first time.

I had made arrangements to stay with my great-aunt, who stayed hunkered down in Kabul long after most of the family had left the country. My first stop was my family's mattress shop to meet her son, Waheed, and my father, who happened to be in Kabul on business, for lunch.

The road to the shop meandered past the places that would sustain me over the coming weeks: butcher shops, kebab stands, spice markets, teahouses, and bakeries. Afghans have a powerful relationship with bread. My grandfather wouldn't start a meal until there was bread on the table, and he insisted that we end every meal with at least a small morsel of it. He would say it was *naane-e-shukur*, or "bread of gratitude," a reminder of

those periods of war and unrest, when meat and produce were scarce but bread was for the most part a constant, and brought some semblance of normalcy to daily life.

I was greeted at the shop first by Waheed and then by the unmistakable smell of simmering *shorwa*, a quintessential winter stew of beef, beans, and root vegetables. Stacked neatly next to the communal bowl was a mound of freshly baked bread and a raw onion. My father, who had returned to Afghanistan fairly regularly after the fall of the Taliban, had told me that he began each trip with a meal of raw onion and bread to steel his coddled American stomach. He made sure that I would do the same. Like many things I would encounter in the coming days, lunch was all about surrendering to ritual.

My great-aunt's apartment was in the Macroyan neighborhood, a densely populated Soviet-built block in the eastern part of the city, true to its era in its architectural starkness. As I made my way through its narrow corridors, signs of the approaching holiday began to appear: coarse bristles against bare concrete floors, the rhythmic thud of broomsticks against old rugs being beaten over balcony rails, the clamor of pots and pans. Kabul was readying itself for Eid-e-Qurban.

Growing up, I had always found it difficult to explain Eid-e-Qurban to my non-Muslim friends. Owing to the lunar calendar, it always fell on different days, and it didn't have the type of universal recognition of other religious holidays, like Christmas or Hanukkah. I never learned about Eid at school and I never got the day off. It was a holiday that my family observed rather than celebrated, always quietly through phone calls to distant relatives and gatherings among the then-small community of Afghans in New York City. Being a part of that sort of community, you learn the rules for successful assimilation early on:

1) Don't draw attention to yourself; 2) Find common ground; and 3) Downplay anything that has the potential to be misunderstood. For most of my childhood my refrain was that Eid was "Christmas for Muslims." Of course, I knew even then that it was much more. But it was only during this trip that I would be able to experience it as it was meant to be.

Eid-e-Qurban (*Eid al-Adha* in Arabic) is one of several major Muslim holidays. It is a celebration of the story of Abraham, and revolves around the notion of selfless sacrifice to the will of God. As the story goes, Abraham, in an act of submission and self-denial—and upon what he understood to be divine instruction—attempted to sacrifice his only son, Ishmael. Though committed to carrying out his task, Abraham asked Ishmael what he thought of God's command. Ishmael, just thirteen at the time, surrendered to God's will, in his own display of devotion. As Abraham stood poised to cut Ishmael's throat, God intervened, Ishmael was spared, and in his son's place, Abraham discovered a slaughtered ram. In Islamic tradition, we commemorate this extraordinary gesture during Eid-e-Qurban by sacrificing a sheep, cow, or goat.

My family, like many Muslim families in the U.S., didn't usually partake in this ritual sacrifice, known as *Qurbani*. Lack of access was an issue, but I also think that, on some level, we were sensitive to how the ritual would be perceived outside of our community. When I was around five we took a trip during the Eid holiday to visit family friends in Virginia and they took us to a rural farm where a sacrifice was taking place. Even then, my mother made a point of keeping us away from the slaughter. Most years, we would pay our local Afghan butcher in advance to have an animal sacrificed in our family's name. We would go and pick up our share of the meat from his shop a few days later. The sacrifice itself occurred away

from our view, so as to negate the possibility that we were ever going to be in a position of having to explain it.

For Muslim Americans, it is impossible not to be aware of—or, really, to be assaulted by—the perception of Islam as a religion of brutality and barbarism. Images of civil wars and sectarian violence in places like Afghanistan, Iran, and Iraq in the 1980s have given way to the graphic beheadings and unthinkable cruelty that permeate the media today—the work of false prophets and sociopaths on the fringes, all of it having a chilling effect on true expressions of faith. For many Americans, the ceremonial sacrifice of livestock as part of a holiday celebration comes with the fear of being misunderstood or maligned. Even writing about Eid-e-Qurban means fighting against a compulsion to downplay or conceal it.

The morning of Eid began much like every other morning I spent in Kabul. I was awakened by the call to prayer echoing through Macroyan's cement corridors. The brutal cold and the lack of heating in the building made it impossible to fall back asleep.

But breakfast was somewhat less routine. Indulging in my morning ritual of tea, bread, and cheese from an Italian-run canteen at a nearby military outpost, I found myself distracted by the pained cries of livestock outside. By midmorning, the blood of sacrificed animals moved like rainwater through the shallow gutters behind our building.

There was a small courtyard behind our apartment, one of the few patches of grass, albeit frozen, that I had seen anywhere in Kabul. From the kitchen window, I could see the aftermath of the Qurbani that had already taken place in the courtyard. Steam rose from the bloody ground, ropes used to tether the animals still hung from tree limbs, and butchers resharpened their knives in preparation for their next engagement. It was a scene that I would see repeated in small alleyways, side

streets, and front yards throughout the city.

For our part, my family had pooled together money for a cow to sacrifice for the holiday. As Waheed and I headed out of the apartment that morning, my great-aunt, who hadn't said but a few words to me thus far, handed me a large, tattered burlap sack. "For the head," she said in Dari. "I promised it to the cleaning lady." And we were off.

Before heading to the warehouse, Waheed and I needed to find a butcher. As it turns out, Eid in Kabul presents an entrepreneurial opportunity for anyone with a sharp knife and a steady hand. After some failed attempts at haggling, we were approached by two teenage boys who offered a fair price and had bikes that would allow them to meet us at the site. The two worked as a pair and split the pay, because neither of them had the strength required to dispatch a steer on his own. Waheed made it a point to question them on whether they were trained to perform a proper Qurbani. After some further inquiries about their credentials and realizing from their well-used aprons that this wouldn't be their first dance, we made a deal and sent them ahead.

The livestock that had been slaughtered in the courtyard of our apartment complex were relatively small. The animal we had selected would require a bit more space and had been brought to one of my family's mattress warehouses on the outskirts of the city. The steer had been secured weeks ago to arrange for its delivery in Kabul in time for Eid. It had been kept safe, warm, and fed for the last several days by family friends near the warehouse. Islamic law advises that a steer should be fed clean food and water prior to being slaughtered. According to tradition, there was already a plan in place to distribute a third of the meat as alms to poor families. As we talked through our various arrangements, I realized that this buildup is what I'd missed out on in America. To prepare for Qurbani is to practice Islam.

By the time we arrived at the warehouse, the boys had already led the steer

out to a small field nearby. We stood there as the boys stropped their blades behind the steer, explaining that they were staying out of the animal's line of sight so as to avoid creating unnecessary fear in its last moments. Their size and age notwithstanding, they turned out to be experienced butchers. I had expected unceremonious violence, but was astonished by the amount of care they took in the ritual.

The final part of the sequence before the actual sacrifice fell to me. One of the boys handed me a bowl that had been cut from the bottom of a soda bottle and asked me to hold it for the steer to drink from. "It's sugar water, so the last thing he tastes in this world is sweet," he told me.

Being implicated in this final act of consideration for the cow's wellbeing hit home more than any other part of the process thus far. Before I could take a step back and reassume my preferred role as passive observer, the taller of the two butchers began to recite the *Tasmiyah*, invoking God's name, and then the *takbir*—"*Allahu Akbar, Allahu Akbar, Allahu Akbar*"—as he firmly took the steer's head under his left arm and swiftly slit its throat.

What I did not appreciate in the moment was that in addition to displaying tremendous skill, these two young boys were also very consciously adhering to the strict requirements for the slaughter (*zabiha*) of animals under Islamic law. The slaughter must occur by hand, using a sharp knife from the front of the neck, through the jugular veins and carotid arteries, causing the animal death by bleeding without severing the spinal cord—precisely what I witnessed.

After being momentarily mesmerized by the heavy rush of blood from the steer's severed neck, I joined the rest of the gathered contingent in trying to gently take it to the ground. It took the weight of all four of us to lay the steer down and hold it still as it bled out. I remember very clearly thinking that, sitting in complete silence on this frozen field next to this dying steer, I felt warmer than I had at any other point during my trip. After several minutes of lying there, each struggling to hold on to a quarter as the steer's muscles involuntarily twitched beneath us, the boys signaled that we could get up.

The main precept of Eid-e-Qurban is self-sacrifice, a notion that is manifest in how the meat is distributed after a Qurbani. Under Islamic tradition, one-third is to be given to the indigent, one-third shared with family and friends, and the final third offered to the party conducting the Qurbani.

Over the course of the next several hours Waheed and I helped with the painstaking process of butchering the steer out in an open field as the temperature dropped. We had promised the boys the animal's hide as part of their payment, so it was understandable that they began skinning the steer with tremendous care. After making a small slit under the skin of one of the hindquarters, one of them placed his mouth over the incision and began to inflate the area. He used a razor to help separate the skin from stubborn spots.

The boys removed the organs and set them aside, then nestled the steer's head into our burlap sack. They expertly quartered the animal by hand. Waheed and I were given knives to assist. We separated the meat into green plastic bags in three equal piles on three corners of a frost-covered blue tarp. Under the watchful eyes of our young instructors, we took special care to make sure that each pile had its equal share of choice cuts.

Save for a few small bags for shorwa and kebabs, we ended up placing most of our share in the pile to be distributed to the poor. We finished dividing the last of the meat as late afternoon approached, and parted ways with our butchers.

Joined by my father, we loaded the meat into taxis and headed for what was described to me as a small encampment of displaced people on the edge of town. What we found was a small city constructed by row upon row of crudely repurposed metal shipping containers, some housing multiple families seeking refuge from the cold.

We walked beside the taxis as they moved through the camp, pulling meat from the vehicles and passing it out to waiting hands. I noticed that it was mainly children who would come close enough to take the meat, while the adults—almost always a father or an uncle—would stand just close enough to thank us and say *Eid Mubarak*—"Blessed Eid"—a reminder that Afghans never take a holiday from pride or grace.

Within minutes we had given out almost everything we had in the cars, including most of our own share. I could see a large crowd of people fanning back out from the road into the grid of containers with small green bags in hand. It was an incredibly humbling and gratifying moment.

As an early dusk fell on Kabul, we started our long, silent drive home. My great-aunt, knowing that we would be coming home hungry and cold, had planned to cook us shorwa for dinner. She had freshly baked bread and was just waiting on the meat, which we delivered. Dinner was served on an old tablecloth laid across her living room floor. It was one of the more extraordinary meals I've ever had. Like most other nights in Kabul, it was too cold to really sit up for much beyond one final pot of green tea and cardamom shared among the four of us.

I slept that night with the steer's head underneath my bed. After nearly thirty years, I finally had my own holiday story to tell and my own memory of Afghanistan to share. I haven't been back since that trip, but not an Eid has gone by that I don't know exactly what I'm missing. **LP**

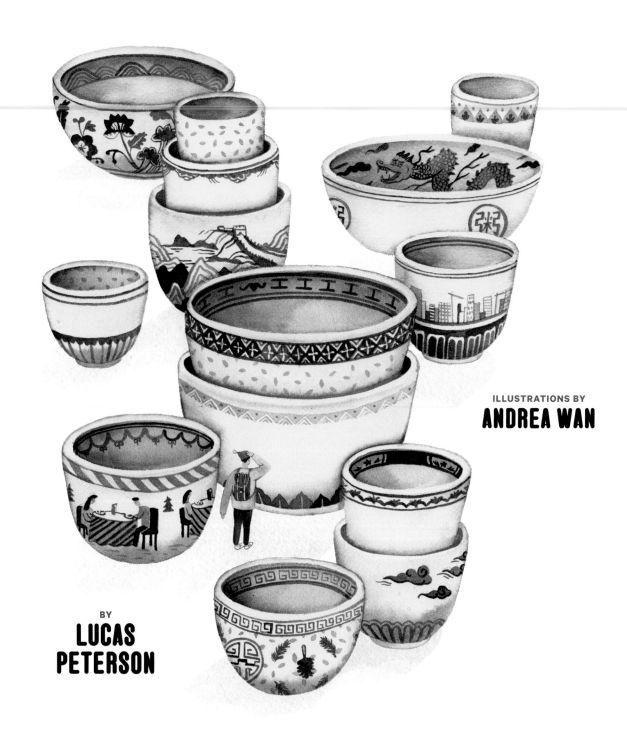

ILLUSTRATIONS BY
ANDREA WAN

BY
**LUCAS
PETERSON**

DEUS X-MAS CHINA

The Friday before Christmas, Robert Young, my manager at the Holiday Inn Downtown Beijing,[1] told me that there should be one more box of Christmas ornaments in a storeroom in the basement somewhere, and since I wasn't busy, would I mind looking for them? I looked, not that thoroughly, in between boxes of promo materials for the hotel's Indian restaurant and some banners celebrating a nonspecific hospitality award before going back upstairs to tell Robert I couldn't find them.

He grinned a big, toothy, lonely grin, and put his arm around my shoulder, no mean feat for someone a full ten inches shorter than me. My fellow employees mocked Robert and called him *luobo zhang*, a nearly homophonic insult they made up that meant "turnip stamp" in Mandarin, which for some reason was really cutting and hilarious. Robert was

unmarried, pushing fifty, and faced the double-whammy social handicap of being 1) aggressively nice, and 2) Cantonese, which made him automatically suspicious to most Beijingers. In accented English, he said, "That's okay, man. I just really love Christmas, you know?" He lowered his voice conspiratorially and added, "They don't know how to celebrate Christmas here." I squirmed away from him to clock out and catch a cab to the east side of town, the Sanlitun neighborhood, where I had another job as a bartender.

Robert was right that they didn't do Christmas very well in Beijing, which only made sense, really, given the official lack of Christians. The Chinese Communist Party is atheist and only even officially acknowledges the *existence* of five religions—Buddhism, Taoism, Islam, Protestantism, and Catholicism—so it might have been a bit naive to expect much hall bedecking and jingle belling. At the McDonald's or Kenny Rogers Roasters down the street, there was cursory acknowledgement of the holiday via hasty decorations or maybe a special menu item. Foyers of Beijing satellite offices of American multinationals had sad, corporate-mandated trees or some tinsel strung on the door; maybe a mannequin in a Santa hat on the sidewalk. But no one was buying

anyone else presents, and no one was getting time off from work. Christmas was, for the city's ten million inhabitants, just like any other day.

This came as something of a culture shock to me, a half-Chinese teenager from suburban Chicago. My family didn't much go for religion and, come to think of it, we didn't much go for being Chinese, either. That was fine with me, as my being the only Asian kid in class had its fair share of horrors. I had a friend named Joe who liked to say he was a "cafeteria Jew." Well, we were cafeteria Swedish Asians—we mulled over our choices before picking and choosing those aspects of our heritage we liked most. Like many American families, we were content to be a mash of different traditions: on New Year's, we did champagne toasts with the neighbors but also engaged in potsticker production of Foxconn-esque proportions. Cabbage- and onion-chopping stations were run in shifts, overseen by my mom. No food processors were allowed, and when chopping onions got too difficult on the eyeballs, we poked holes in slices of bread and strung them on our faces as masks. We looked like something between Secret Squirrel and carbohydrate cosplay enthusiasts, but it stopped the stinging.

On Christmas, we did the Rockwellian turkey, just like everyone else,

[1] International Holiday Inns are not the same joyless budget hotels as those in America. In other countries, these are fine establishments, on par with your Hiltons or Sofitels. There were three Holiday Inns in Beijing in 1997. I had just turned nineteen and was working at the least fancy of the three. We were not the Crowne Plaza, in the ultra-luxe Wangfujing shopping district, nor were we the Lido by the Beijing airport, which was (and still is) the largest Holiday Inn in the world. No, we were the unmarried, horse-faced older cousin, with 300 rooms, a small business center, and a chip on our shoulder.

but our interest in the bird was somewhat disingenuous. The meat was the price we paid for the real treasure: five pounds of ossified protein, collagen, ragged bits of meat, and marrow that provided the DNA for a good batch of *jook*. It all went into a large pot with water and rice, some scallions and ginger, maybe carrots and onions. Simmered and thickened overnight, and my week between Christmas and New Year's was instantly mapped out: an endless cycle of napping on the couch, not shoveling the sidewalk, consuming bowl after bowl of jook, and masturbating to the three-breasted hooker scene in *Total Recall*.

Teenagers have an enormous capacity for self-contradiction, and I was no exception. I loved our Christmas jook tradition, but part of me felt contempt for it. I instinctively and enthusiastically consumed gallons of jook—the living room was littered with empty bowls of it—but would altogether eschew it if my white friends were around. I would demonstratively decry its FOB-iness; the word *jook* looked so much like the slur *gook*, it made me cringe, and it nagged at me as a reminder of the permanence of my feeling alien in my hometown. It was built in, and something I could only attempt to escape. When I left for Beijing to work at the Holiday Inn (taking a leave of absence from college due to poor grades), it was almost certainly for the purposes of executing some half-baked, *Roots*-y vision quest. And it took me about a week to come to the realization that, damn, I felt even *more* out of place in China.

Housed in an old converted theater, just beyond the Beijing Workers' Stadium, was the Success Club, where I worked when I wasn't at the Holiday Inn. It was one of countless fly-by-night clubs, places that operated in legal limbo for eight or nine months before the police would eventually catch wind and shutter them. Success was the outfit of the moment

when I moved to Beijing, extremely popular with expats.

I said hi to the owner, a young Ukrainian woman named Olga, and made my way through the crowd to the makeshift bar, which was just a few tables laid out end to end. "Everybody (Backstreet's Back)" was playing, people were dancing, and an Australian guy in a Carlsberg beer shirt had just punched a different Australian guy in a Carlsberg beer shirt. A pretty typical start to the night.

To describe what I did as "bartending" would be extremely generous. I poured pints from a keg of Tiger beer and made drinks where the ingredients were spelled out in the name. Jack and Cokes abounded. Toward the end of the night, a woman I'd seen before was standing at the bar, nursing one of my signature gin and tonics. I spun my best line at her in Mandarin: "Hello. Have you eaten this evening, or not?" She replied, "Can you make me another drink? This one is too strong." We shouted at each other for a while over the music. She was from Beijing and her name was Lina. She usually had a fat white guy with her, but tonight she was alone. Her black hair was pulled back tight, and she was wearing a pair of rimless gold glasses and a white fur wrap. She kept looking down at a Nokia candy-bar cell phone. She said that she had to go meet someone. "How about you take me out to a nice dinner next week?" she asked.

We settled on the following Thursday, which was Christmas Day. That was my idea. I needed to do something that day, with another person, to take my mind off of being alone and to thwart the depression that was slowly rolling in like fog. After three months in Beijing, I'd hit a wall. I worked diligently through my little Chinese textbook in the evenings, yet still no one understood me. I caught a cold and filled dozens of tissues with streaky black mucus; the bad air, hazy and thick with coal soot, was getting the best of me. And I was tired of looking for excuses

not to hang out with Robert, who, earlier that week, while changing clothes in the office behind the front desk (something he'd been asked not to do), was pestering me to hit up the Christmas buffet with him over at the Swissôtel. I'd heard it was a pretty awesome buffet, but I didn't think I could handle Christmas with Robert.

I did like the idea of having an "American" Christmas experience, however, and that was how Lina and I ended up back in Sanlitun at TGI Fridays on Christmas Day. She seemed very happy with the choice (American chain restaurants are always *en vogue*), and I was hoping that some drinks, a fajita tower, and some holiday flair could shoehorn something, no matter how ill fitting, into the absence I was feeling very deeply.

We were well into our evening before I figured out that Lina worked as a high-priced escort. I asked her who the men were whom she usually showed up with at the Success Club, and she said, "No one. Business. So tell me, is America really dangerous?" I pushed her on the issue and she squared up, glared at me, and said, "Look, do you really want to know?" I didn't say anything for a few seconds, just looked down at my bright blue drink, and then she continued, "Are you really from Chicago? Al Capone, right? And Michael Jordan!" The waiter came over with our food: ribs for her and some soggy penne thing for me.

I asked her where in the city she lived, and she wordlessly produced her *shenfenzheng*, her national ID card, and used both hands to pass it to me. I could read none of it, but could make out her age, thirty-one, a dozen years my senior.

I was nineteen and still a virgin, and had an overwhelming obsession with sex mixed with a deep fear of actual physical contact with the female body. I was mostly afraid of her once I figured out she was an escort. She treated me alternately with bemusement and extreme irritation over my poor Mandarin. "But aren't you

Chinese?" she asked more than once. "Chinese is so easy," she said, sucking on a rib and signaling the waiter for a refill of her Long Island iced tea. We continued to graze and, by the time the check came, it had become the most expensive meal I would ever eat in China—by far. It blew my food budget for weeks. I also felt ill afterward; maybe it was from the sticky Jack Daniels glaze, or maybe the "Jingle Bell Rock" Muzak on endless repeat. Either way, this wasn't the fake, secular Christmas I wanted. I wanted a genuine approximation of my family Christmas, goddamnit.

She lived close to the restaurant, and after I paid the bill, we walked to her building. She didn't invite me up but wordlessly held the door open for me, and I went in, up four flights of stairs, and into her one-room apartment. "Be quiet," she said, pointing. In one corner of the room, her son, who looked about seven, was sleeping; in the other, a woman who looked to be in her eighties. A couple of white bedsheets were hung from ropes attached to the ceiling, used to cordon off different parts of the room. She said, "What's with you, are you sick?" I nodded yes. "Diarrhea?" I said no, not that. She motioned for me to sit at a small table in the kitchen area. She poured me a glass of warm Sprite from a bottle that was in a cupboard above the sink. "I'll give you a bowl of *zhou*." Jook. "That always helps."

She went to a big pot on a two-burner gas stove sitting on the counter and ladled out some grayish jook into a red-and-white plastic bowl. It was thicker than we had it at home. I thinned it out a bit with some sesame oil and vinegar, but I didn't take more than a few bites. I told her I couldn't eat the rest of it. "What's wrong? Don't you like jook?" I said of course, I love jook, we eat it all the time at home. "Then what's wrong?" I don't know, I said, it's just not the same. I think I'm just full. "*Aiya*," she sighed as she took my bowl away, and put it on the counter. "You Americans. You really are a *huai dan*." A spoiled egg. My retort, the

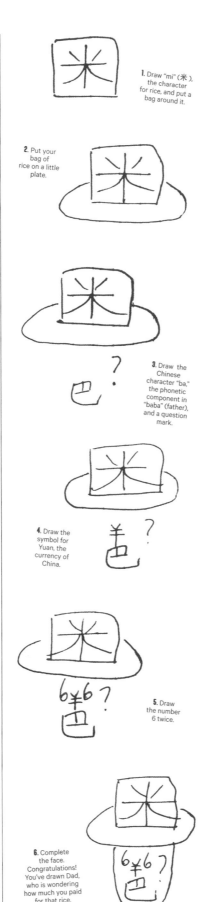

1. Draw "mi" (米), the character for rice, and put a bag around it.

2. Put your bag of rice on a little plate.

3. Draw the Chinese character "ba," the phonetic component in "baba" (father), and a question mark.

4. Draw the symbol for Yuan, the currency of China.

5. Draw the number 6 twice.

6. Complete the face. Congratulations! You've drawn Dad, who is wondering how much you paid for that rice.

best I could come up with, was, "*Wo bu shi yige huai dan.*" I am not a spoiled egg. She snorted. My inability to volley with a snappy comeback annoyed me, more so than her insult. I stood up from the table to go but she said, "Wait, wait—you're not a *huai dan*. I'm sorry." She smiled and motioned for me to sit back down, and I did. We sat there, the sounds of sleep filling the room, while I finished my Sprite.

After about a minute, she took a pen out of her purse and said, "Hey, have you ever seen this before? This is a lot of fun," and spread out a paper napkin on the table. She drew the Chinese character for *rice* and began to recite a poem in a voice one might use to tell a fairy tale to a child: *Wo you yi dai mi*, which means, "I have a bag of rice." With each line of the poem, she drew another character and added to the drawing.

Wo you yi dai mi.
我有一袋米.
Fang zai pan zi li.
放在盘子里.
Baba wen wo, "Duoshao qian?"
爸爸問我, "多少钱?"
Wo shuo, "Liu shi liu."
我說, "66."

I have a bag of rice.
I put it on a plate.
Father asks me, "How much did it cost?"
I say, "Sixty-six."

There was a face when she was done, drawn out of Chinese characters. She asked, "Isn't that funny?" I said yeah, that was really cool. Dad, wearing a Panama hat, very intent on knowing how much you paid for that bag of rice.

I asked Lina if I could try, and she gave me the pen. We recited the little ditty together, and I did the drawings. The first few times were rough, but eventually I got the hang of it. I could recite the whole thing without her help, and soon my drawings were indistinguishable from hers. **LP**

CUP OF CHEER

DRINKS BY JIM MEEHAN
ILLUSTRATIONS BY MONICA RAMOS

JIM is throwing a Christmas party to show off the sumptuous recent remodel of his mountain ski chalet. He's invited friends, financial advisors, three responders to a Casual Encounters post on Craigslist, and two men both claiming to be Santa Claus. Rather than warm tidings or holiday cheer, the mismatched menagerie of guests has brought neediness, thirst, and a host of individual anxieties. Fortunately, Jim is none other than Jim Meehan, bartender par excellence and proprietor of PDT in New York City, and, one by one, he mixes up customized liquid remedies for all.

1. After inadvertently veering off course during a routine ski run, **MAX** was forced to dig a snow cave and inhabit it for eight days. The man needs a warm après-ski cocktail.

2. **SANTA #1** is having trouble convincing anyone of his identity, because he's not plump enough. He's on a steady diet of carbs and egg yolks.

3. **SANTA #2**'s diet of milk and cookies has made hurrying down the chimney nearly impossible. If he's ever to pop out of a fireplace again, he'll need a drink that's easy on the waistline.

4. Peter invited nine-time Wimbledon champion **MARTINA NAVRATILOVA** to the party under the pretense that there would be a cocktail called the Martini Navratilova. Who would have thought she'd actually come?

5. Poor **CATHERINE** slipped on an icy sidewalk last week and bumped her head. She's just recovered from a bout of temporary amnesia and realized she has her own party to host tomorrow night. She needs a recipe she can serve to a crowd.

6. SABRINA and AL are on their first date, and Al's breath is absolutely putrid. Can we get this guy a breath mint?

7. JESSICA and AMANDA's flight to Hawaii was canceled. Now they're stranded here for Christmas. A tropical cocktail might cheer them up.

9. MABEL's accompanied by her disapproving mother-in-law. Her husband, Tom, says that Mom frowns on drinking liquor, but is okay with wine. Mabel needs something a little stronger in her cabernet if she's going to make it through the night.

8. MAILMAN RYAN has to work on Christmas, but that's not going to stop him from having a cup of good cheer. He just needs to be able to carry it in a flask.

11. As the party gets into full swing, the booze reserves dwindle. JIM runs out to restock but finds that all the Christian-operated liquor stores in town are closed. Just as he's about to lose all hope— wonder of wonders—he spots a specialty Jewish booze emporium. Christmas is saved! Thanks, Jews!

10. BETTINA's new boyfriend has celiac disease, and she's sworn off gluten in solidarity. But she desperately misses gingerbread cookies.

1. VERTE CHAUD
Serves Max

4½ oz	hot chocolate
1½ oz	Green Chartreuse
+	heavy cream, whipped to soft peaks

Combine hot chocolate and Green Chartreuse in a warmed glass. Top with whipped cream.

2. COFFEE COCKTAIL
Serves Santa #1

1½ oz	Martell V.S.O.P. Cognac
1½ oz	Noval Black Port
¼ oz	simple syrup
1	large organic egg
+	nutmeg

Combine everything but the nutmeg in a cocktail shaker and shake. Add ice and shake again. Strain into a chilled coupe and garnish with grated nutmeg.

3. WHISKEY HIGHBALL
Serves Santa #2

2 oz	Yamazaki twelve-year-old Japanese whiskey
3 oz	club soda
+	mint

Combine whiskey and soda in a chilled Collins glass filled with ice. Garnish with mint leaf. Serve with a steel straw.

4. MARTINI NAVRATILOVA
Serves Martina Navratilova

1½ oz	Hendrick's Gin
¾ oz	Dolin Blanc Vermouth de Chambéry
½ oz	Pimm's No. 1
1	cucumber slice

Stir gin, vermouth, and Pimm's with ice and strain into a chilled coupe. Garnish with a slice of cucumber.

5. WINTER WASSAIL*
Serves Catherine and friends

1¼ oz	Tariquet V.S.O.P. Armagnac
½ oz	Kronan Swedish Punsch
1 t	St. Elizabeth Allspice Dram
4 oz	**Wassail**
1	cinnamon stick

Add the spirits to a preheated mug. Top with warm Wassail and garnish with a cinnamon stick.

*Created by Jeff Bell

WASSAIL
Makes 18 servings

½ gallon	Hudson Valley Cider from Breezy Hill Orchard, or any good-quality apple cider
2 C	orange juice
½ C	lemon juice
12	cloves
4	3"-long cinnamon sticks
½ t	ground ginger
½ t	ground nutmeg
4 oz	Armagnac

Simmer everything but the Armagnac on medium-low for 45 minutes, then fine-strain and cool. Add Armagnac and store in the fridge. Reheat before serving.

6. STINGER
Serves Al's bad breath

2 oz	Paul Beau V.S.O.P. Cognac
¼ oz	Tempus Fugit Spirits Crème de Menthe
+	mint

Stir the spirits with ice and strain into a chilled coupe. Garnish with a mint leaf you've smacked between your hands.

8. BOULEVARDIER
Serves Mailman Ryan

1 oz	Rittenhouse Rye Whiskey
1 oz	Martini & Rossi Rosso Sweet Vermouth
1 oz	Campari
1½ oz	water
1	orange twist

Combine whiskey, vermouth, Campari, and water in a flask. Chill in the freezer before pocketing. Garnish with an orange twist.

10. GINGERBREAD MAN
Serves Bettina

2 oz	Banks 7 Golden Age Rum
¾ oz	The King's Ginger
½ oz	Grandma's Molasses syrup (1 part Grandma's Molasses, 1 part water)
1 t	Dale DeGroff's Pimento Aromatic Bitters
1	organic egg white
+	cinnamon stick

Combine everything but the cinnamon in a cocktail shaker and shake. Add ice and shake again. Strain into a chilled coupe. Garnish with grated cinnamon.

7. PAINKILLER
Serves Jessica and Amanda

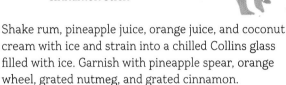

2¼ oz	Pusser's Rum (Myers's Rum Original Dark also works well, but a true Painkiller® must use Pusser's)
1 oz	pineapple juice
½ oz	orange juice
½ oz	coconut cream
1	pineapple spear
½	orange wheel
+	nutmeg
+	cinnamon stick

Shake rum, pineapple juice, orange juice, and coconut cream with ice and strain into a chilled Collins glass filled with ice. Garnish with pineapple spear, orange wheel, grated nutmeg, and grated cinnamon.

9. NEW YORK SOUR
Serves Mabel

2 oz	Wild Turkey Rye Whiskey
¾ oz	lemon juice
¾ oz	simple syrup
½ oz	full-bodied red wine or port

Shake whiskey, lemon juice, and simple syrup with ice and strain into a chilled rocks glass filled with ice. Float the red wine or port over the surface.

11. MANHATOWITZ
Serves both Jews and Gentiles

2 oz	Concord Grape Manischewitz
1 oz	Clear Creek Slivovitz
2 dashes	Angostura bitters
1	grapefruit twist

Stir Manischewitz, Slivovitz, and bitters with ice and strain into a chilled coupe. Garnish with grapefruit twist.

ADAM GOLLNER

VODOU HOLIDAY

Papa Legba, ouvri baryè pou li;
tou mistèr gider li.

Papa Legba, open the gate for him;
let every mystery guide him.

-VODOU CHANT

Thousands of pilgrims had assembled in Limonade's main square on a sun-stained summer day. Dusty masses descend upon this beverage-named village in northern Haiti each July 26th to honor Grande Sainte Anne, a goddess revered for her benevolence and wisdom. Like other deities in the Vodou pantheon—known as *lwas* in Creole—Grande Sainte Anne is venerated through offerings, particularly the making and eating of food. She is not to be confused with another aspect of the same lwa, named Ti Sainte Anne,[1] who is called upon to mete out revenge, even murder, on behalf of those who've been wronged.

Many of the *vodouisants* in attendance were taking some downtime, having walked long distances to be here and danced until dawn. Devotees were sprawled all over the place—sleeping on park benches in the shade, on the ground beneath *mapou* trees, on the back of

---

1 "Small Sainte Anne" as opposed to "Great Sainte Anne."

motorcycles. Some were napping on the pews in the town's church and on its cool stone floor, while more awake believers murmured and gesticulated and cried toward the pulpit, imploring Grande Sainte Anne not to withhold her favors over the coming year.

Outside the gleaming white church, Vodou dolls covered in sequins were for sale next to terrified-looking live chickens, soon to be sacrificed, that had been crammed sideways into too-tight buckets. Vendors sat under tarps

hawking murky potions and *ouan-gas* (charms). It was hard to tell what exactly these consisted of. During his travels in Haiti, the journalist William Buehler Seabrook (1884–1945) documented the making of a love ouanga in which pulverized hummingbird powder and wildflower pollen were mixed with dried blood and the semen of a person seeking love, then sewn up into a pouch made from the desiccated scrotum of a goat.

A root gatherer[2] sitting over a pile of bark and twigs gestured for me to come closer. Putting down his plastic bottle of *kleren*—a homemade rum moonshine—he lifted the lid off an old tin box. A serpent glistened within, coiled up, writhing. Its forked tongue flicked out like pink lightning. The medicine man quickly closed it back up and started laughing. A hypnotized-seeming woman next to him stared at me through expressionless eyes the color of clouds, taking a long, serious drag on her cigarette.

"To understand Haiti you have to experience deep Haiti," said my underworld guide, Emmanuel Arry Brignol, a Vodou researcher and archivist who has spent the past three decades documenting ceremonies across the country. "And this, *mon cher*, is deep Haiti." It wasn't the chaotic bustle of Port-au-Prince, he meant, nor the pastoral calm of Haiti's countryside villages. It was high noon on the one day of the year that pilgrims from all over the country arrive in Limonade to celebrate Vodou mysteries. Deep Haiti.

Brignol believes in Vodou, but more than a practitioner, he is an observer. As we spoke, a few women walked past us carrying chairs on their heads. They wore fiercely proud looks on their faces. Brignol said he'd seen them a few nights earlier at a fire ceremony. "There was a large bonfire and these people were dancing inside of it, in the fire," Brignol continued, excitedly.

"They were able to take the heat fine, no problem. They were dancing in the flames." The lwas like to purify themselves in fire, he explained. They descend into human hosts, making them take red-hot coals into their mouths or roll around in burning embers. One of the unexplainable verities of Vodou worship is that those in the throes of possession don't feel any pain in seemingly lethal scenarios.[3] Anyone mounted by a lwa becomes capable of doing things only a god should be able to do.

It felt like we too were dancing in flames as we walked though Limonade. The day was so unrelentingly hot that sheens of sweat had soaked through most of my clothes. Everything chafed. I nodded in sticky agreement when Brignol suggested that we stop for lunch. He brought me to a three-seat, corrugated-tin shack just off the main square. The establishment, called Lortina, wasn't so much a restaurant as a one-pot soul food soup kitchen, like the handful of other joints in town. The floor consisted of plywood planks draped over an open gutter. Diners throw their fish bones into the ditch below through cracks between the boards. Haiti has no wide-scale sewage system anywhere in the country, let alone here in the remote north.

As basic as the setting was, the food at Lortina was fit for a lwa: we feasted on *pwason gwo sèl* with *labouyi bannann* and *diri kole ak pwa rouj* (whole red snapper and boiled plantains with rice and beans). Over lunch, Brignol told me that he started

---

[2] Or *doktè-fèy*, as they're known here, meaning "leaf doctor."

[3] Beliefs have been shown to interact with endorphins in fascinating ways. Endorphins, the body's self-generated opioid painkillers—referred to as "the poppy fields of the mind," by the biostatistician R. Barker Bausell—spring into bloom in the presence of pain, spicy food, or extended physical activity. (Hence the term "runner's high.") According to fMRI scans, devout Catholics have a higher pain threshold when they are administered low-level electrical shocks while simultaneously being shown images of the Virgin Mary. Their religious contentment turns off pain receptors and kicks the poppy fields into action. Some form of this effect may provide an explanation for what occurs to "temporarily unhoused" bodies in Vodou possession.

studying Vodou after university, "bit by bit penetrating into the different secret societies" until finally they allowed him to start filming their rituals. "It took a lot of time and a lot of patience," Brignol concluded, reminding me that my own attempt to learn about the role of food in Vodou would likely require a similar commitment.

Still, I'd come at an auspicious time: many important ceremonies take place at the end of July. Besides the Grande Sainte Anne event already under way, this week also marked the feast day of Maitresse Silverine, who, according to the one description of the ceremony I could find online, "only very slightly tastes of the food offered to her," as well as the beginning of the Carnival of Flowers in Port-au-Prince, which doubles as a celebration of Maitresse Lorvana, a lwa who is sustained by the scent of flowers. On top of that, the *fête champêtre* of Saint Jacques Majeur had just ended the day before.

Saint Jacques Majeur is known as a soldier of Papa Ogou, the lwa of war, the spirit of fire, the "bloody, dreadful one whose voice is thunder." "The Africans who came over here had to call him Saint Jacques to appease their European masters, to camouflage his true nature," Brignol explained. "But everyone knows that Papa Ogou is the true lwa behind the name of the Catholic saint."[4]

Ogou's ceremonies take place in Plaine-du-Nord, a short drive away from Limonade, where each year a large basin naturally fills up with muddy springwater. Bathing in the mud pit is said to be good for the soul, so people of all ages dive into the mucky brown pool, emerging caked in healing clay. Some vodouisants throw money, food, or rum into the mud to propitiate Ogou, but a more significant display of gratitude is the ritualistic sacrificing of cattle.[5] (Sheep and goats may also be used, but Ogou has a soft spot for cows.) The animals are sacrificed both as a way of thanking the god for his assistance over the past year, as well as a means of sending him nourishment.

The sacrifice is a lengthy procedure. First the cow is bathed, then perfumed, powdered, garlanded, and fitted with finery. After being paraded around the village, it is brought back to the mud pit, where it is fed and given rum. A priest—called a *houngan*—asks the creature whether it is ready to be received by Ogou. Then, to the accompaniment of drumming, a machete comes out. The bull's neck is slit quickly. Blood runs into the mud. An intensely fresh smell fills the air. As the lwa feeds upon the spirit or life energy of the cow, a transubstantiation occurs in which the god enters into the animal's blood. The leader of the ceremony plunges his knife into the bull's heart, collecting the god-filled blood into a calabash bowl. The participants then drink this blood, transfusing the lwa into themselves, and enter ecstatic trances. The houngan sprinkles the remaining blood over the devotees until their white robes turn crimson. Blood is painted onto faces, possession occurs; people become Ogou. They start hurling themselves across the mud pit, some even swallowing broken glass or sticking razors into their skin.[6]

Watching this frenzied communion, an outsider might recall that Christians, too, drink the blood of their god, although in a more sanitized, less carnal fashion. Forget wafers and wine. In Haiti, they go whole hog—fat, gristle, and all. After the taking in of the spirit, the rest of the animal is then cooked and shared with others attending the ceremony. "Sharing is a very important part of the ritual," Brignol told me. "You share the meat with others, with strangers. The idea of giving is central to Haitian animal sacrifice."

Ogou and Grande Sainte Anne aren't the only lwas given food. "It's the same with all the other lwas—they're all fed by their followers," the Haitian-born, Montreal-based publisher and poet Rodney Saint-Éloi told me shortly before I traveled to Haiti. "In the invisible world, just like in the visible, eating is always above all in Haiti." Some of the lwas have a fondness for peppermint, others favor offerings of bananas, cabbage, peppers, turkeys, or preserved fish. Agwe, the spirit of the sea, is fed in dazzling fashion: floating white tablecloths covered with fruits of all colors are sent out to her on the surface of the sea.

Wade Davis has written of how, in the nineteenth century, an apparition of the Virgin Mary materialized atop a palm tree in Ville-Bonheur. The country's Catholic Church saw this miracle as an opportunity to convert pagans to monotheism, and promptly consecrated the site with a chapel. Their excitement turned to dismay, however,

---

[4] King Louis XIV's *Code Noir* banned all African non-Christian religions from being practiced in Saint-Domingue, as the colony was then known. Some scholars assert that as a result, the transplanted slave population disguised their lwas as Roman Catholic saints—a blending that became known as syncretism. Just as Ogou and Saint Jacques are two references to the same divinity, Grande Sainte Anne (mother of the Virgin Mary) can be seen as a syncretistic way of saying Grandma Erzulie. Following independence, Haitians didn't discard their Catholicized spirits; instead, they kept them among their firmament of deities, and have continued honoring them to this day.

[5] From the Q and A section (*Category: Animal Sacrifice*) of a website addressing common misconceptions about Vodou:
Q: "I am a vegan and I don't agree with the eating and killing of the Gods'/Goddesses' creatures. Does this mean that this is not for me?"
A: Yes. That is exactly what it means. Incidentally, it is not what you believe that is important. It is what the Gods/Goddesses demand that is the most important.

[6] Examples of such possessions abound in Wade Davis's ethnobotanical study of Haitian Vodou, *The Serpent and the Rainbow*, which concludes at the Plaine-du-Nord mud pits. In 1929's *The Magic Island*, W.B. Seabrook wrote of witnessing Ogou possess a follower as worshippers were singing a song about Ogou being hungry and thirsty. Seabrook felt as though it were the lwa himself devouring the sacrificial meats and fruits arrayed for him on the altar. The man kept shoving huge handfuls of cake into his mouth, drinking long gulps from a wooden vessel filled with congealing goat blood, and otherwise binging like a god of war preparing for battle, looking completely unaware of his surroundings.

when the Catholic priests started finding offerings of food at the Virgin's shrine. Vodouisants believed that it wasn't the Virgin Mary who'd shown herself in the palm fronds, but rather Erzulie Freda, lwa of love.

Despite colonial efforts to extract and squash it, Vodou remains integral to Haitian culture. The war of independence—the only successful large-scale slave revolution anywhere in the world—is said to have begun with a Vodou ceremony held in the summer of 1791. The gathering took place in a hidden knoll at Bwa Kayiman, about a thirty-minute drive away from Limonade. "The ceremony was officiated by a Muslim Egyptian from Jamaica named Boukman Dutty," Brignol explained. On the night of August 14th, a priestess sacrificed a black African pig to the lwas. Lightning struck. The priestess was possessed by Erzulie. Everyone present joined a blood pact to fight for the country's freedom. The movement grew from there, taking on momentum, and by 1804, following a protracted series of battles with France, Haiti had liberated itself from colonial rule.

That's part of the reason Vodou remains so revered in Haiti today. What is erroneously called "Voodoo"[7] has a reputation of being bound up in evildoing. In truth, witchery, pincushion dolls, and zombie-slaves are only a small part of an immense—and immensely complex—spiritual worldview. Vodou certainly entails making appeals to the gods to do your bidding, and feeding them to do so, but at its heart Vodou is a religion concerned with the possibility of establishing connections between this world and that of the lwas.

---

[7] This spelling is today considered obsolete and disrespectful of the actual religion. The word *Vodou* comes from either a Fon word referring to "the divinity of the Fon pantheon" or the Ayizo term for "mysterious forces or powers that govern the world and the lives of those who reside within it." The religion's roots can be traced back to the Kingdom of Dahomey (now Benin), although it also incorporates indigenous religious traditions as well.

"Have you been to Haiti before?" I asked the airline attendant en route to Port-au-Prince.

"Oh yes, often," he answered. "Many, many times. I can't even count how many times."

"And do you like it there?"

"Sure, I guess—although I've never been off the plane."

It took a moment to compute. "Oh. So you've flown to Haiti many times, but you've never actually stepped foot in the country?"

"That's right. We're not allowed to deplane. The airline's insurance company forbids it. Haiti is just too dangerous."

Dangerous though insurance agents may consider it, Port-au-Prince is also one of the most fascinating cities on earth. The capital's technicolor streets are filled with people selling whatever they can: coconuts, hubcaps, plastic baggies filled with potable water, eggs, articles of clothing. Everybody is out in the streets. Most of the stores in the city are right there on the sidewalks. You don't go to the mall in Haiti. You buy your shoes on the street the same way you buy your plantains or your photocopy machines. When you need a mattress, you go see the mattress guy with his mattresses resting against a wall. The whole city

is an outdoor market. Everywhere you look you see caged peacocks or giant vats of bubbling millet or people carrying weighty baskets on their heads.

Alongside its lack of a sewer system, Haiti also has a lot of garbage on the side of the streets. Heaps of it, often on fire or decomposing languidly in stagnant rivulets of blue-green sewage. The smells of Port-au-Prince veer between cerebellum-stingingly miasmic and magnificently floral. Throughout the day, notes of mangoes, coffee, and jasmine pierce through the acrid fumes of pollution and smoldering trash. Instead of NO SMOKING signs, there are lots of NO GUNS signs, as well as metal lockers into which one can stash his or her Glock while entering an arms-free establishment. I asked my driver in Port-au-Prince, named Abner Zephyr, whether Haitians often carry guns on them. "Of course!" he responded, as though I were crazy to ask.

On my first morning in Haiti, I met with Richard Morse, leader of the influential *mizik rasin*[8] band RAM. He came to Port-au-Prince in 1985. "I arrived here looking for Vodou ceremonies, so I could find the Vodou rhythms," he recalled over breakfast. At the time he moved here, he'd been playing in a punk band from Princeton called the Groceries. "We played at CBGB a bunch in the early '80s. I wanted to be doing world music, though, and someone gave me the idea that 'if your mom is Haitian you ought to go to Haiti.' I never went home."

Morse is a serious yet mellow dude, a tall, imposing vocalist whose long, white, frizzy ponytail gives him a bit of a tropical Arlo Guthrie vibe, but with more attitude. "The Vodou rhythms brought me here, but what I learned is that those rhythms don't walk alone," he told me. "They have steps, spirits, ceremonies, melodies, messages, meals, and more. So I came here looking for one little thing and I got this whole lifetime of knowledge

and experience that's been handed down for centuries and centuries and centuries."

Morse's mother is the Haitian singer Emerante de Pradines, while his father was a Yale professor descended from New England Puritans who arrived in Massachusetts in 1635. "You know, we have a Vodou-type celebration in the U.S. every year," he said. "When I say that, everyone thinks 'Halloween.' No. I'm talking about Thanksgiving. It's an offering to the spirits of agriculture. In the past, they would've sacrificed the turkey. Now they buy it ready-made at the grocery store. You have the squash and the pumpkin and the beans and the corn and the cranberries. These foods are for the spirit of agriculture. In the States, you give your prayers and say thanks for a moment before you eat, but here there's singing, dancing, drumming, music, and prayers that go on for quite a while, even up to a week sometimes. People rejoice here, sure, but what they really want is for their prayers to be answered."

As we spoke, Morse pointed up to a painting on the wall above us. It showed around twenty or so lwas crammed in side by side, enjoying a banquet at a long, low table. "All the spirits receive offerings of food," he explained. "When you have a ceremony, you put their food out in a special place and then the rest of it is separated among everybody else."

Morse and I were sitting on the front porch of his hotel, the Oloffson, one of the weirdest and most interesting hotels in the world. There's a Vodou shrine at the main entrance. At its front is a statue of a man with the body of a coiled-up snake: Damballah, the sky god, primordial creator of all life. On the wall above him hangs a wooden *objet* implanted with various body parts hacked off a black doll, its limbs crowned with the skeletal remains of some kind of fish or bird. Another doll hangs on the wall, clutching a bloodied machete, surrounded

by a violent farrago of rusty nails. Not the typical decorative flourishes of a boutique hotel. Inside, the walls are covered with Vodou art, much of it as beautiful as it is disconcerting (think paintings of demon-like creatures, or of a burial rite in the countryside). The employees in the reception area are seated behind a wooden counter so high that only their eyes and upper heads poke out above the top of it. The hotel itself is falling apart, but in a magnificent way. *Rickety* is the operative word. "Some people like it here and some people don't," Morse muttered, with a punkish shrug.

When Morse first arrived, he got a day job here as an assistant manager. He took over the lease shortly thereafter and has been "living in a fantasy," as he puts it, ever since. "As soon as I got settled here at the hotel, I set up the band. My wife, Lunise, opened up the door for me to get access to the local culture. She was dancing in a local folklore troupe. I added instruments to that troupe and we turned it into a band. And now the hotel has become a *lieu* for Haitian culture. That's how we approach it, whether it's the placemats, or the sculptures, or the food. It's a cultural experience that we do here. You should try the goat."

The two best-known dishes in Haiti are *griot* and *tasso*. The latter consists of goat, beef, or turkey marinated in the juice from the country's famous bitter oranges.[9] Griot is a supremely satisfying fried pork dish usually served alongside *bannann peze* (flattened, fried plantains) and *pikliz*, a spicy, tart and utterly addictive condiment that somehow fuses coleslaw into hot sauce with a kind of lime-relish effect. Since discovering it, I now eat pikliz with many non-Haitian dishes as well. It deserves to be famous the world over.

---

8 Roots music.

9 Haitian oranges are the key flavoring ingredient in Grand Marnier, Cointreau, and Marie Brizard.

There are numerous other specialties, from guinea hens with cashews or walnuts to *legim*—a thick, flavorful mash made primarily with eggplants, mirliton, cabbage, and other vegetables, sometimes served with crab. *Riz aux djon djon*, a blackened rice dish made with the country's indigenous black djon djon mushrooms, is as amazing as the country's basic rice and beans, also known as *riz national*, or national rice. Stews like *tchaka* and *soupe giraumon* are emblematic of Haitian history and are connected both to the slave uprising and to the lwas.

Over the past two centuries, Haitian cuisine has managed to successfully incorporate different global influences. Just as the country's religion is a syncretistic combination of different backgrounds, the cooking here combines traditions from their indigenous population, from their African past, from France (the use of dairy, notably),

and from their other early European colonizer, Spain. They've also been shaped by later waves of immigration: notes of German, American, and Peruvian cookery can be detected in contemporary Haitian food. A large Italian population in the nineteenth century led to spaghetti becoming an unlikely breakfast food in Haiti today (it is often served with smoked herring). Perhaps the most unexpected dishes in Haiti's general repertoire are those with a Middle Eastern influence, a development that can be traced back to the waves of Lebanese and Syrian migrants that started settling here in the mid to late 1800s.

As a result, visitors to Haiti can now eat *lalo*, a dish of braised greens and meat made with Middle Eastern molokhia leaves, or *kibi*, a Creolified version of Lebanese *kibbeh*, those ground-meat torpedoes. Kibi are the specialty of the house at Observatoire

restaurant, located on a promontory 3,000 feet above sea level in Port-au-Prince. It is the perfect spot to have a fresh cherry juice while sitting overlooking the entire sun-sparkling city and its turquoise harbor. But be prepared: it's windy up there. While I was waiting for my kibi to come out, the wind blew the tablecloth off my table and it lay there quivering on the floor like a deflated ghost with pepper-shaker eyes.

The owner of Observatoire, Marie-Claude Gabriel, came out to speak with me. "What Haiti needs is better publicity," she said. "Not the chikungunya,[10]

---

[10] Chikungunya is a non-immunizable, mosquito-borne fever that has rapidly spread all over Haiti. Its name comes from the East African Kimakonde language and means "contorted or hunched over from pain." Chikungunya causes searing arthritic discomfort throughout all the body's joints: knuckles, elbows, knees, back, hips, neck. Wherever you move—if you can actually stand up, that is—you feel it. A friend who'd gotten it in Haiti had been

which just came this summer—and from where? It's not from here! Just like the U.N. brought cholera. Everybody who writes about Haiti focuses on the poverty, the poverty. Sure, but nobody ever speaks to the guy selling socks or avocadoes all day long on the side of the road. That's their life, and if you ask them, they'll tell you they're happy doing it, even though they can't go home at the end of a day to watch *television*." (She nearly spat this last word out, as though it were the foulest venom on earth.)

According to the U.N.'s World Food Programme, malnutrition is an endemic problem in Haiti, where about 38 percent of the population lacks access to potable water, and around 55 percent of the nation lives on less than $1 per day. Still, Haitians know how to do a lot with a little, especially when it comes to food. Locals often eat quite well despite their circumstances. "Haiti is a complex society that an outsider cannot judge too quickly—they would be mistaken," the writer Dany Laferrière told me. "Food is very important in Haiti, and getting food can be difficult for the poor. Still, all people have access to lots of good fruits and vegetables. There are ways to eat more than you'd think—it isn't linked to salary. It's linked to what the earth proposes. The thud of a mango falling off its branch is something you hear often. I only eat mangos and avocadoes when I'm there."

I discovered my love for Haitian food at a place in Montreal called Marché Méli-Mélo. It's a lunch counter in the back of a store filled with Haitian groceries, beauty products, CDs, and books. Méli-Mélo serves what Rodney Saint-Éloi calls "grandmother food." "Exile is loss, the loss of the self," he told me when we met there for lunch before my departure to Haiti. "But there are

places that bring you back home without a plane ticket. Here at Méli-Mélo you live what you live in Haiti on any street. This is people's childhood. They come here to rediscover it in the odors of the lost country. Méli-Mélo keeps it all alive symbolically."

According to Saint-Éloi, everything in Haiti comes down to food. "Eating is the paramount collective fantasy, the primal dream: what will we eat? Haitians say it in the morning: how will we feed the kids? Then they dream about it at night. They dream of what they don't have. The imagination of the self and others passes through food. Our country is built on the esthetics of manducation. In all spheres, eating is the most used verb and the most effective metaphor. In politics, we eat our enemies—we *bouffe* them, we make them disappear. If you say you are going to make love to a girl in Haiti, you say you are going to eat her. The mosquitoes, they don't sting you in Haiti—they *eat* you. Haitian literature is one of the few in the world where all the characters are always eating. We write how we eat: we have insatiable appetites. Because we have nothing. The idea of 'too much' doesn't exist. They took everything from us; there is no 'too much.' I don't know any Haitian who doesn't love eating. Meals in Haiti are always big celebrations—they eat, they sing, they dance. Eating is a party. There are no portions. You're always given enough food to feed three. And Haitians will finish everything on their plate—because they're never sure when they're going to have their next meal."

When the Europeans arrived, Haiti was a very different place than it is now. Columbus wrote of how it was the most fertile land under the sun, how it was entirely void of pestilence, how abundant the supplies of freshwater were, and how the trees reached up to the heavens.

Today the country is considered synonymous with deforestation, lack of safe drinking water, contagion, and barrenness. Much of that is due to the way the Europeans treated this land. Columbus famously described the island of Hispaniola to Queen Isabella by grabbing a piece of paper, crumpling it up, and then tossing the angular jumble onto the table in front of her. His point was that it is a

bedridden for a week, wracked with intense joint pain. Even now, months later, he still can't go to the gym, as his body can't handle the exertion. "As they say in Haiti—*ça cogne fort*," he told me. (It knocks you hard.)

topsy-turvy landscape of mountains and valleys. The unfortunate consequence of that gesture is that the country ended up being treated like something you'd throw into a wastebasket. Over the next three centuries, this island became the most lucrative colony in the Americas, a place they would keep plundering and exploiting over and over and over. The tragedies that occurred here are inconceivable.

One way to begin understanding how the country got to be the way it is today is by visiting the Museum of the Haitian National Pantheon. The institution serves both as a commemorative edifice that recounts the history of Haiti's origins as well as a sarcophagus containing the final spiritual remains of the country's founders—the former slaves Toussaint Louverture, Henri Christophe, Jean-Jacques Dessalines,

and Alexandre Pétion. Their mausoleum consists of a circular array of tombs floating in blue light.

The most interesting rooms in the museum are those dedicated to the slavery period and the revolutionary period. From the beginning, the African slaves brought over by France were determined to preserve their cultural and religious identity. Despite being forbidden from practicing their faith or from playing their music, they found a way to incorporate their gods into a monotheistic paradigm, worshipping lwas as saints. They also managed to preserve their African drumming traditions. "This is the drum called the *assoto*," my guide told me. "*Assoto* means 'to call the ancestors.' Yes, this drum was used in Vodou, and was instrumental in the resistance, the gathering together, and the fighting against the French."

The next room contained the bell of freedom Toussaint Louverture rang in 1793 to herald the emancipation of the country's slaves. The French didn't give up without a fight; they continued attacking Haiti's revolutionaries over the next decade. In the end, they lost tens of thousands of veteran soldiers—and their colony. The Haitian blue and red flag was created when Jean-Jacques Dessalines took the French flag and tore the white section out of the tricolor and had it sewn back together. Here was the first indentured country ever to overthrow their subjugators, and they massacred them.

Having deposed their masters, the leaders of the Haitian resistance started dressing like French generals, wearing tight silk pants, tasseled boots, and long-tailed coats with ruffled sleeves. Soon they declared themselves kings, queens, even emperors, donning ermines and puffy gold crowns set with ludicrous quantities of precious gemstones. They built opulent palaces and fortifications, like Sans Souci palace and citadel, a UNESCO heritage site I would visit with Emmanuel Brignol a few days later.

One oft-overlooked detail of the truce with France is that Haiti agreed to pay France 150 million francs to compensate them for lost revenues and possessions. They were forced to take out immense loans—with bloated interest rates—to cover these payments. By the end of the 1800s, 80 percent of the country's national revenue was going toward repayments of loans compensating France. Despite

having freed themselves from the fetters of slavery, they still remained exploited for generations—right up until America occupied the country from 1915–1934, in large part to ensure Haiti's continued debt payments to France, at that point embroiled in the costly First World War. Then came a series of dictators, some of them propped up by the U.S., all of which culminated with the earthquake of 2010, which took the lives of 220,000 people and injured another 300,000 or more. It remains among the gravest natural calamities of our lifetimes.

That extraordinary history has had the effect of making the people of Haiti deeply resilient. Even if they've lived more misfortune than most nations, their culture remains intact—and the rest of the world is now committing serious resources to helping the country move forward.[11] While now is the perfect time to see Haiti as it once was, change is coming swiftly, and it will be fascinating to see where things go over the coming decades. As the artist Frankétienne wrote me, a few hours after I visited him at his painting-filled home in Delmas:

"We've become tightrope walkers and virtuosos of the crises that have undermined us and exhausted us. In recent times, the West has fallen into a succession of financial, economic, political, and social crises of their own. But the current global crisis is one of culture and civilization. Take care, my dear Western friends, to not sink to the bottom of the abyss on this descent to hell! Poor little Haiti could well become the professor who will help you surface. Our long experience as secular victims is a major trump card."

[11] Many of the country's debts were cancelled after the earthquake, in attempts to support recovery efforts; since then, hundreds of millions of dollars in foreign investment have entered the country, mainly aimed at developing Haiti's tourism infrastructure. The United States government has also provided $4 billion in relief assistance intended for longer-term recovery, reconstruction, and development programs.

On the evening before I departed from Port-au-Prince to Limonade and northern Haiti, I couldn't find the key to my room at the Oloffson anywhere. I looked for forty-five increasingly aggravating minutes, unpacking all of my bags, and then finally giving up. I went down to the front desk without locking the door, in the hopes that they would be able to give me a replacement. Before agreeing to do so, they sent me back up to the room for a final look, with a young maintenance guy named Mackabou.

"You must have lost the key because you are too tall!" he joked, chuckling slyly as he walked through the room. "Or maybe the key is too small? Could it be that it dissolved in the shower?" He was full of ideas. But within two minutes, he found the key under the pillow of my made bed.

"It means you need to listen to your dreams," Mackabou declared, becoming serious now, as he held the key up to the light. "The key is under your pillow; the answer is in your dreams." He then started doing a dervish dance next to the bed.

To unwind from the frustrating key search, I decided to take a dip in the Oloffson's pool—I'd spotted a couple bathing in it earlier. When I got a closer look, I saw the pool surface was deeply murky, oily even. It was covered in feathers, spiders, dead flower blossoms, and thorny branches topped with extremely sharp points. It was a suitably freaky pool, its water almost milky. I dipped my feet in. The water was as warm as a hot bath—and about as hygienic as a mosquito spawning pond. After a few minutes, I decided to just dive into the broth, to stop being afraid of chikungunya and malaria and cholera and everything else the doctors had warned me about. Submerging my head under the stewing surface, I had the sensation of entering a cauldron. Being cooked alive is probably the only way to really experience a place like Haiti. Just give yourself over to it; it'll melt your flesh regardless.

That night, I dreamt that my shadow found a way to unburden itself of the weight that had been keeping it tied down, that had been preventing it from being who *it* truly was, and my now-boundless shadow self soared off into the darkening air to rejoin its source: the night.

I felt this to be a good thing. At the same time, I also had the perturbing sensation that I shouldn't be feeling anything.

When this happens, I told myself, you aren't supposed to feel it, you aren't supposed to be aware of it happening—let alone be conscious in any way at all. This decoupling took place on a stone path leading up a mountain, and I watched it happen from the comfort and constraints of a country-style wooden coffin that swayed back and forth like flotsam on waves as it banged against the pallbearing knees and hips lugging my shadowless, still-feeling corpse toward its final resting place in the hills.

In Haiti, when storytellers begin a tale, they first check with the audience to see if they're ready by asking one word: *Krik?*

If you want to hear the story, you respond: *Krak!*

There's a moral to every story in this country. Often, it comes down to an ancient Creole saying: "*tout moun fèt pou mouri.*" It means: "everyone must die," or "we were made to die."

Haiti is a place where corpses can be used for magical purposes, a place where mirrors are still considered passageways to the realm of the dead. Vodou is sometimes referred to as a "death cult." It's more accurate to characterize it as a religion that *reveres* death—like most other religions, of course. Vodou teaches adherents that when they die, they will be reborn in some form or another.

The basic precepts are as follows. Our body is called the *corps cadavre*. It is animated by the *n'âme*, a life force that remains in a corpse as it decomposes. This is complemented by the *z'étoile*, one's astral counterpart, a part of us up in the sky, our star of destiny. We all have two souls, the *gros bon ange* and the *ti bon ange*. The former, the "big good angel," returns to God immediately upon clinical death. The latter, the "little good angel," spends one year and one day in a purgatorial space among *Les Invisibles* or *anba dlo*—under the water. These spirits emerge after their sojourn beneath the rivers and then find their way to the branches of trees. "If you listen closely," writes Edwidge Danticat, "you may hear their hushed whispers in the wind."

One of the characters in the Haitian author Gary Victor's *13 Vodou Stories* talks about the way each of us constructs a symbolic universe in order to make sense of a world that makes no sense. If that's the essence of what Vodou is, one could also say the same of writing—of whatever it is we do to modulate the experience of having been thrown into this inexplicable existence.

In Limonade, I found myself having a conversation with a *bokor*, or priest, about the secrets of nature. We were seated beneath a tall mapou tree. He himself had planted the tree here, he said, long ago. One time, when he was tired, he came here and slept under it and enjoyed it. "And when I am dead I will still enjoy it," he continued, "when I become a butterfly or a bird, I'll fly around its leaves. Even if I become a fly, I will enjoy it. Or a little ant, climbing up its trunk."

Some friends joined us; we spoke about truth and happiness. We could write an entire book under this tree, the priest said. We all fell silent for a moment, sitting there in the shade of the mapou tree. "Listen!" whispered the bokor. "*Le chant des cigales...* You never hear cicadas singing like that

in Port-au-Prince anymore." A black butterfly spiraled around in front of our group for a moment. Someone started saying that black butterflies bring misery. "That's not true," the bokor interjected. "Sometimes they bring good fortune. You can't know. It's a mystery. *Tout est animé...* all is animated. We shouldn't say it's a *mystery*—we should say it's *exceptional*. Because mystery is normal."

After lunch at Lortina, Emmanuel Brignol suggested we check out a nearby sanctuary. "It's a Maroon locality, a zone where African slaves who'd escaped were taken in by Taíno Indians," he continued. "The ceremonies there have always been mixed between Taíno and Vodou traditions."

Leaving the town center, we drove up a dirt road to the top of a hill. The path was lined with dagger-sharp cacti and thorn-covered aloes. We passed a group of naked children covered in thick paint-like coatings of soap, scrubbing themselves at a public shower. At the end of the road, a sign informed us that we were at LAKOU DEREAL. A lakou is a kind of sanctified open-air courtyard in the countryside.

"This lakou is very powerful," Brignol told me as we walked in. The lakou was an open space with a few ancient-looking trees scattered around a small bungalow-style temple. Near this mystery house, some kids were playing with each other and several elderly women sat drinking coffee. "Lakou Dereal has always been a sacred place," Brignol continued. "It is in a strategic area, surrounded by mountains. Sometimes a huge serpent can be seen walking around inside the temple."

As that image settled to the bottom of my thoughts, a woman came out to greet us, a calmly intense barefoot priestess in an ankle-length robe. Her fingers were covered with gemstone rings. She wore her eyeliner in an ancient Egyptian style. "This is

Ingrid Llera," Brignol said, introducing us. He told her that I was an ethnological writer interested in the role of food in Vodou.

"Very good," she responded, nodding slowly. "It is only by understanding food in Haiti that you can begin to understand Vodou. There are big misconceptions about Vodou—that it is evil; that it is witchcraft; that it is black magic; that it can kill you. Everything that is bad and ugly. But in reality, it's the contrary. When you study Vodou, you learn to see nature."

Llera placed a hand on the trunk of a locust tree. "Vodou is about coexisting with nature," she continued. "All life-forms, all material objects, all phenomena are manifestations of God. God is in everything; God *is* everything. That is why we respect all life. That is why we feed the lwas. And that is the true essence of Vodou."

Llera told us that she is what's called a *serviteur*—one who serves the lwas. To *serve* is to participate in the back and forth between the worlds. "I am the chosen one from this lakou," Llera explained. "My mother was a priestess as well. And my uncle was a priest. My father was a Cuban Santeria practitioner who worked in a sugar refinery. My mother, she is a peasant from around here."

The following day, she told us, would mark Lakou Dereal's annual ceremony honoring all the gods in the region. I was welcome to attend—on the condition I be purified ahead of time.

"How does that work?" I asked.

"You come into the temple and you will see," she replied.

She indicated that I should enter the *hounfour*. A hunched-over, wizened old woman with cataract eyes stood there in the gloom. She was holding a brown ceramic jug filled with water and a single lit candle. "Fire and water," she declared solemnly, bowing at me eerily. I took my hat off and bowed back. She led me toward a stone mound with a column of wood sticking out of it in the middle of the room. "This place is in between life and death," the lady explained. "This totem is called the *poteau-mitan*. It represents the force that sustains. For us, it is the center of the universe. It connects this world to the spirit world."

She handed me the ceramic jug and told me to pour three sips of water onto the mound. "While you do it, ask the spirit for any favor that you would like," she said. "Ask with freshness. Ask with respect. Ask for peace, union, love—whatever you want. Give the spirit water. Water is life."

She then led me into the next room, the sanctuary. "This is the room

reserved for the entities," she said in a hushed voice. As instructed, I took my shoes and socks off before entering. The dirt on the floor was soft and crumbly. It felt good to stand in it. There was a low table in front of me, covered in unfamiliar objects. She pointed out a few of them: a rusted ankle chain from the slavery era; bird feathers; a toy pony; a Taíno headdress. There was also an archaic six-pronged pitchfork, traditionally used in animal sacrifice.

She told me to pay my respects to the elders. I did so, pouring water onto the floor three times. It ran through the loose, dusty soil, coagulating into mud which caked itself onto my feet. I imagined ghost tongues licking at my toes.

Llera joined us in there, uttering a prayer, and then directing my attention to the left front corner, where a dozen or so small clay pots of different sizes sat. "These are the spirits of children—our children who have not yet come, our children who are still out there," she said, pointing to the distance, through some many-colored flags. "The children are spirits somewhere, floating in light, waiting to be born."

"Send them a message," the older woman implored. "Send your future children your love."

I took a deep, nervous breath. "Can't wait to meet you," I said inwardly, sending my as-yet-unconceived children my love.

Then we walked over to the back left corner, where more pots, of a bigger, darker nature, were clustered. "These are the gods of masculinity, of virility, of power, of warfare," Llera exclaimed. "Pay them your respects, and ask them for might." I poured out three sips of water and asked them for might.

We moved to the back right corner, where the female energies could be found. "These are all the Erzulies," Ingrid said. "This is where love, grace, compassion, gentleness, warmth comes from. Ask them for undying love."

I did so.

Next we came to a higher table in the back of the room, covered in perfumes, candles, alcoholic spirits, incense. Ingrid took the jug from me and asked me to cup my hands. I did so, and she filled them with water. "Now pour this all on your head and your spirit will be cleansed," she commanded. As I poured the water over my head, the light in the room seemed to change colors. The old lady clapped her hands and cackled loudly.

"And now," Llera announced, clinical as a dentist, "you have been *purified.*"

The following dawn, Brignol and I went back to Lakou Dereal for the ceremony. We arrived just after sunrise. Llera hadn't slept since the day before. "I was up all night," she explained. "The ceremonies in Limonade were so nice I couldn't leave."

Her assistants offered us Creole coffee with freshly made *manioc* bread that had been toasted on a large round heated stone out front. "This is Taíno-style bread," she explained. "Passed on from the Indians to the Maroons to us today."

For breakfast, we all ate steaming bowls of *soupe pain*, or bread soup. It was made with stale, dried-up bread and a host of vegetables. "They put herring in it, hot peppers, bread, onions, thyme, garlic, water, carrots, celery root, spinach—whatever they want, really—then they add the leftover bread and mash it up." As unlikely as it sounds, it was deeply satisfying—smoky, savory, and spicy, a bit gluteny, but the perfect food for when you've stayed up all night long at a Vodou festival and you're about to celebrate another one.

The rest of the morning went by uneventfully. Some drummers showed up. Emmanuel Brignol greeted old friends. Llera went about her preparations, using ground manioc to trace *vévés*—geometric drawings representing lwas in Vodou liturgy—in a circular shrine she set up in the middle of the lakou.

Around noon, a group of ladies walked in dressed entirely in white. They were led by a radiant woman wearing an imposing ruby ring and a bigger headdress than the rest of her troupe. "I call the members of our *société* my herrings," she explained. "I am their *mambo*. Mambo means mother, high priestess, the person in charge—like Ingrid."

Her name was Marie Carmele Lubin Mentor, although she told me that her *nom vayan*—"like a *nom de guerre*, but a *nom de Vodou*"—was

Satela Bonmambo. She and her herrings were from a nearby temple, called La Société Legphibao. "The goddess that we offer to is called Philomise," Bonmambo told me. "She is more or less an aboriginal goddess. She can be found at the waterfront near Limonade. She has been there *depuis toujours*... since forever."

"And what sort of offerings do you make to her?" I asked.

"Various things. She likes candy, actually. Also fruits. When we give fish to Philomise, we give her a plate with other side dishes as well."

For lunch, we had one of the best and simplest meals I ate during the course of my week in Haiti: *maïs moulu avec feuilles de campagne*, or ground corn cooked with country greens and spices. It was magnificent, somewhere between a risotto and a polenta, entirely of that place. Several women had been boiling the dried corn down, stirring a large, bubbling cauldron constantly, over the past couple of hours. Llera explained that the meal was itself a consecrated offering, sacred food meant for sharing with the gods, with their ancestors, and with the community at large.

I ate alongside a group of newcomers—some pilgrims, as well as a nonbelieving Haitian woman who'd come along for the experience. As we drank tea, a man in a bandanna mentioned that it's important to tap tea bags three times and utter prayers before steeping them. "It will bring you boons," he assured the others.

"Well, I make tea with the flowers from my garden, so that idea doesn't apply to me," said the agnostic hanger-on.

"You should do that with the flowers in your garden as well," he retorted, frowning.

"But I don't want to tap them," she insisted. "I love the flowers in my garden, but I'm happy smelling them, clearing the garden, watering them. Just doing that lifts my spirits."

"It's because you touch them," he said.

"Yes, but I'm not going to tap them."

"You should."

"*You* should! You are allowed to tap things, but I'm also allowed to not tap them. I don't want to start tapping my flowers *or* my tea leaves."

The ceremony finally got underway. We all filed into the temple where I'd been purified. Small lit candles were handed out to each of us. Ingrid started by welcoming us. "We are the resistance," she intoned, speaking about how this ceremony would give people an idea of what real Vodou is, not the falsifications that have been described abroad. She started singing a song in praise of Legba, the guardian of the gates, the lwa found in between this realm and the other. Singing to him encourages him to open the barrier between the world of the visible and the invisible. Pretty soon, others joined her in song, shaking rattle gourds filled with snake vertebrae. As they did so, a bat suddenly flew in the room and started careening around erratically. A *bat*! In the middle of the day. In a Vodou temple. Fluttering around our heads. What's next, I wondered, ducking as it swerved through the otherwise unperturbed congregation: Will an immense serpent walk over and join in on the chanting?

Wax from our candles dripped onto people's hands, shoes, my notepad. The ladies dressed in white each picked up a colored flag, as did Ingrid's followers. The bat kept flying back and forth all furry and befanged. The drummers led us down to the front gate, where they sang more songs and held their flags up, welcoming the spirits in. They then started pushing their flags up against each of the trees in the lakou, spending a few minutes on each tree, singing and dancing. It seemed like they were trying to awaken the spirits within, to break through to an experience of them, asking them to flow through the flagpoles into their collective energy. Whatever they were hoping for, it worked. A lwa arose, possessing an elderly lady. She started shivering and quivering, quaking and shaking. *"The curtain has been lifted,"* the worshippers sang, ecstatically, riding the syncopated rhythms of the drums, *"the lwas have come."*

Much more took place after that, but as Ingrid Llera told me, there are certain things that the profane cannot disclose, let alone witness— even those who've been purified. To fully partake in these rituals requires becoming initiated, a process which consists of isolating yourself in a sacred chamber for nine to seventeen days alongside twenty-one "superior spirits." That would need to wait for another time.

For now, I had a flight to catch, back to Port-au-Prince, where the Carnival of Flowers was set to begin. All the gathered-up anticipation seemed to have condensed itself into the sky. The evening's celebrations were just getting underway when the rains came. The crowds quickly thinned out of the grandstands and the vibe fizzled palpably. It wasn't quite what the minister of tourism described in one of her columns in *Magic Haiti* magazine as "an outbreak of contagious gaiety [that] incites vigorous waving of hands, fits of joy, and in some cases spontaneous gyration." Instead, a team of muscular daredevils was pulling wheelies on ATVs, splashing onlookers and intimidating the tentative clusters of merrymakers below.

Within minutes, the initial torrents turned into an *avalasse*: a pounding tropical storm. Ducking into an alcove to escape the lightning, I felt terrifically dismayed—not for myself, but for all the locals. It had been so hot and stifling for so long and then on the big night everybody's been waiting for and preparing for and working on for weeks, the whole mess gets rained out. A young guy next to me in the doorway looked like a sealed envelope that had been steamed open by someone other than the intended recipient. "It's over," I sighed to myself, around nine p.m., and retired to my room.

Trying to read in bed, I started thinking morose thoughts about the incessant hardships and obstacles this place has faced, and continues to face. But, as Frankétienne reminded me, one should never underestimate the core quality of Haitians: resilience. When I ventured out again, a couple of hours later, attracted by the noise outside my window, I quickly realized how entirely wrong I'd been. It was still raining hard, but the party was raging even harder. The storm hadn't stopped anyone.

Soaking wet, hundreds of thousands of revelers were *ra-ra*-ing in the streets. Fireworks were going off like machine guns. As the mambos had emphasized: water is life. The platitudinous thought arose that—this being a carnival of flowers—there would be no flowers at all without rain. Gradually the storm tapered off. By midnight, it was a memory. All it had really done was cool things down a few degrees and washed away the dust of the preparations so the main event could begin. The storm seemed in retrospect like a benediction from up on high.

Pretty soon, the sound systems started coasting by, truck beds covered three stories high in speakers blaring superfast beats. People danced, girls made eyes at boys, fights broke out. The police swung batons through the crowd, but nothing could dampen the celebration. Who cares what the rest of the world thinks, the streets seemed to be shrieking, who gives a witch's tit about natural disasters, dictators, poverty?

As the night went on, each oncoming float banged out rhythms faster than the ones before them, to the point that it didn't seem possible to imagine music ever getting any more accelerated than this, *vrrra-vrrra-btap-btap-ki-ki-ki-ki-btap-btap*, the whole wild mass as frenetic as frenetic gets, the air geometric with decibels surging from the masses of speakers, rainbow steam rising off the masses of grinding people, confetti drifting through the sound waves massed in the night sky. Everyone seemed possessed. Here a Baron Criminel, there a Maitresse Lorvana. Ogou, Erzulie, Loco, all of them, everywhere. To an onlooker caught up in the almost tangible glow of the saturnalia, looking up at the color bursts exploding in the sky, it didn't feel too difficult to imagine actual gods out there somewhere looking down on this and smiling devilishly at each other as they ate it all up. **LP**

WHEN (FOOD) MOUNTAINS WALK

—

BY **MELATI KAYE**

PHOTOGRAPHS BY
BUDI DHARMAWAN

Soup, rice, maybe a piece of tempeh or fried egg: a feast fit for a king, at least if that monarch happens to be Sampeyan Dalem Ingkang Sinuwun Kangjeng Sri Sultan Hamengkubuwono Senapati ing Ngalogo Ngabdurrokhman Sayidin Panatagama Khalifatullah ingkang jumeneng kaping X, the plain-living inheritor and appointed governor of Yogyakarta, on the Indonesian island of Java.

Three times a year, though, the sultan's palace chefs get to prepare something rather more extravagant—a cordillera of "food mountains": elaborate mounds of rice, capped with rice cakes and green beans, flowers and chilies. The chefs will craft seven in all, each mountain piled high on a palanquin and paraded by liveried porters down the main thoroughfare of Hamengkubuwono's princely domain. These aren't so much for eating as for revering and then demolishing in

a frenzied free-for-all food fight.

Traditionally, the sultan's palace is venerated as the spiritual axis around which the Javanese cosmos spins. Hamengkubuwono's worshipful subjects pour into the city from all around Yogyakarta's volcano-ringed basin to participate in the ceremony.

The palace chefs spend around four days painstakingly preparing the food sculptures, called *gunungan,* from the Javanese word for mountain. At the end of the parade, it takes the crowd barely five minutes to reduce the ornate confections to mere rice crumbs.

The gunungans symbolize a well-ordered universe. Celebrants believe that to win a slice of the cosmic cake is to ensure good harvests, pay raises, and romantic success in the months ahead. Hence the frantic scramble to score a piece.

"Hide it, bury it, fry it up, and eat it. Really, you can do anything you want with these talismans," says Pane, one of the palace servants working in the ceremonial kitchen.

In contrast to this free-and-easy approach to consuming the demolished food mountains, the rules for producing them are punctilious in the extreme. The gunungans must embody the harmonious balance of their

surrounding milieu, according to Professor Marsono, who teaches Javanese culture at Yogyakarta's Universitas Gadjah Mada, one of Indonesia's foremost academies.

The ratios and placement of ingredients piled onto the three-and-a-half-meter-high food mounds stay the same from year to year. The recipe cannot vary, regardless of such unpredictable occurrences as floods,

volcanic eruptions, bumper crops, or poor harvests. That, Marsono explains, is because the gunungans are meant to restore the cosmos to an idealized and invariant baseline equilibrium: "They function like computer reset buttons."

Nowadays, the reset is scheduled three times a year to correspond with Muslim religious benchmarks: the prophet Muhammad's birthday (Mawlid), the end of the fasting month (Lebaran, aka Eid al-Fitr), and the festival to commemorate Abraham's willingness to make a holy sacrifice of his firstborn (Idul Adha, aka Eid al-Adha). But by poring over palace literature, Marsono has found that Yogyakarta's gunungan ceremony predates the royal family's adoption of Islam some five hundred years ago. It was even practiced by the Hindu Mataram court, precursors of the present dynasty.

"Religion, rulers—they are like shirts. You always change them," Marsono shrugs. But the gunungan tradition, he explains, is hardwired into the Javanese psyche. It's how they "praise the souls of [our] ancestors."

On the occasion of the prophet's birthday, I join the predawn assembly of the faithful to await the rollout of the rice mountains. The gunungans are stored in a concrete shelter, and the surrounding plaza is packed with rows of minibuses rented by farmers from the countryside. The air hangs thick with the smoke of cooking fires from temporary food stalls. Grandmas lay out traditional snacks on short tables: intestines roasted on a stick, mini quail-egg omelets, and nasi kucing, literally "cat rice," or as one lady clarifies for me, "a cat's portion of rice."

Many Yogyakarta city dwellers don't attend the gunungan ceremony, but the pilgrims from the countryside camp out overnight in the plaza in anticipation of the festivities. At 4:15 a.m., when few urbanites are awake save for late-night partiers straggling home and stray cats fighting on the old city walls,

the villagers rise to watch the rice mountains set forth on the first section of their route through the city.

Today, the parade is late in starting, which gives me plenty of time to inspect the preparations. I find a perch on the steps of one of the gunungan-assembly sheds, alongside Edi, a tobacco farmer who arrived the night before from Temanggung, a village about seventy kilometers away.

This plaza is about as much of the city as Edi and his twenty-one family members (all tobacco farmers) care to see. After the parade and the final frenzied scramble, they won't be staying around for big-city shopping or to take in the sights.

"It's because of the magic," Edi explains. If any of them is lucky enough to grab a sacred morsel, "we must get on the bus and head home or we will lose the magic."

Together we marvel at the detail that goes into the making of each rice mound. The mountains are sexed, says Pane. Edi and I watch as the cooks stud the male mountains with a thick layer of beans. Around the crest of the cones goes a row of teal duck eggs. Five fish-shaped rice cakes form a ring at the top, which is garlanded with jasmine and magnolia flowers. A palace brochure clarifies that this elaborate piling represents the king's relationship to society, his willingness to provide.

As for the "earthly" gunungans, representing females, children, and gender-ambiguous "leftovers," each mountain is populated with 1,500 hidup ("life") sticks, each one skewering colored rice balls that symbolize men (red), women (white), childhood (green), married life (yellow), and justice (black), Pane explains.

Edi and his ilk have every reason to respect the magic of mountains. Like many Indonesians, they live in the shadow of some of the most dynamic mountains on Earth. Four hundred volcanoes dot the country's equatorial archipelago. A seismic map at the Smithsonian's Natural History Museum shows Indonesia as a blur of overlapping red triangles (i.e., active volcanoes).

The gunungan, along with *nasi tumpeng*—adorned rice cones served at all traditional events, from birthdays to weddings to funerals—are perhaps the Javanese's attempt to control their environment through a *mandala*, a symbolic representation of a perfect mountain that nourishes its celebrants, despite its explosive potential.

Edi and I have plenty of time to ponder cosmology, as it turns out, since the parade doesn't arrive at its final destination at the palace mosque for another seven hours. By eleven a.m. the sun beats down on the waiting crowd. The plaza is packed. Families pull out umbrellas and newspapers to shield themselves from the scorching rays. A news photographer ducks under the shadow of a balloon vendor's floating wares.

People press against the palace fence and climb trees to get a better view. A row of police and national guardsmen stand sentry before the mosque where one of the three main gunungan processions will end. (Other termini include the provincial governor's office and the palace of a renegade branch of the royal family.) Even with the front doors of the mosque blocked, plenty of celebrants find their way in through back entrances.

Finally, the gunungans emerge from the palace, preceded by elephants, horses, and a full marching band dressed in Dutch military regalia (a legacy of Indonesia's colonial history). Then comes a contingent of male palace servants, all decked out in starched white shirts, hand-painted batik sarongs, and turbans. Palace porters bring up the rear, dressed in maroon shirts and tall caps.

The porters shoulder the palanquins in relays, fourteen at a time. The male mountains lead the way, each draped in a curtain of green beans. Behind them, the female mountains are shrouded in chiffon-thin, translucent layers of banana trunk. As the hidup sticks bob and sway, the banana trunk becomes a screen for their rippling shadow dance.

With a misguided sense of self-importance, the police toot their whistles and manage to hold back the mob for a little while. But not for long. After the palanquins are set down and a quick Javanese prayer, the crowd surges at the gunungans for the final scrum.

Four men sprint up the sides of the male gunungan in front of me. First one to the top pockets the jasmine flowers crowning the peak (said to grant physical beauty). Then he starts tossing beans and fried rice balls into the crowd.

All hands reach into the air. The whole scene turns into a screaming gridlock. Those who already have a piece are trying to rush away. Those still groping for a crumb push forward. Food flies across the bright blue sky. As the mountain shrinks and thins out, the crowd yanks at the wicker base of the gunungan. The men on top continue to fling clumps of beans into the crowd, utterly unconcerned that their footing is being torn out from under them.

After hardly five minutes, there's no trace left of the deliberate, patterned mandala. Old ladies scratch the ground for stray rice grains. The rest of the crowd fans out through Yogyakarta's narrow back lanes to their parked vans.

A juice vendor steps up to a traffic light, hoping to earn a few *rupiah* from the village-bound farmers. But nobody has time for him. The sweaty, adrenaline-pumped drivers are all too intent on the four-hour drive to rush their magic home while it's still fresh. **LP**

NASI TUMPENG

MAKES 10 SERVINGS (1 MOUNTAIN)

Dodging paper airplanes flung by neighborhood kids, I ducked into Bu Kurma's house. I had come for a recipe, but the de facto catering queen of my Central Javanese community directed me to a feast of sweet tea, fried macaroni balls, and rice steamed in banana leaves. In the sunset hour before evening prayer, she walked me through this recipe, a mini *gunungan* of sorts and the keystone of every meal marking local births, deaths, and weddings.

Try this on a weekend afternoon when you have four or five hours. Substitute the rice-steaming system with a rice cooker, if you're short on time. "But it won't taste the same," Bu Kurma insists. **—MELATI KAYE**

INGREDIENTS

4 C jasmine rice
3" piece fresh turmeric root
    (or 3 t turmeric powder)
1 coconut, grated (about 3–4 C)
1½ t salt
½ t sugar
3 *daun salam* (Indonesian bay leaves), or
    substitute curry leaves or regular bay leaves
3 lemon leaves, or substitute kaffir lime leaves
    or fresh *pandan* leaves (also known as
    screw pine or *bai toey*)
1 stalk lemongrass, crushed/bruised
1 shallot, peeled but otherwise whole

---

1 Soak the rice in cold water for 15 minutes.

2 Grate the turmeric (a Microplane is good for this) onto a square of cheesecloth or tea towel over a small bowl and squeeze it dry. Reserve the liquid.

3 Ideally, you have a woven bamboo cone and narrow pot to steam rice in. If not, set up a steam system with a pot and heat-proof colander/steamer with small holes that fits over the top. Fill the pot with an inch of water, and bring to a boil. Drain the rice, and transfer it to the colander. Reduce the flame to medium, and set the colander on top of the pot. Cover with foil or a lid. (In lieu of steaming the rice, you can omit the grated coconut from the recipe and just put everything into a rice cooker with 4 cups water and 1 cup coconut milk. Cook as you would normal rice, then skip down to step 7.)

4 Steam the rice until half cooked (about 30 minutes over a medium flame, stirring occasionally). Then pour 2 cups of boiling water over the rice and stir.

5 Ladle the rice into a bowl or another pot. Mix in grated coconut, turmeric juice, salt, sugar, bay leaves, lemon leaves, lemongrass, and the shallot.

6 Refill the steaming pot with an inch of water, and place the now-mixed rice back in the basket or colander. When the water is at a rolling boil, nestle the colander back in its place. Cover with foil or a lid, and steam for another 30 minutes, stirring every 10–12 minutes (make sure the colander is covered between stirs).

7 If you don't have access to a 6-inch-wide metal tumpeng cone, make your own with a rolled place mat, or use a bowl or conical strainer. Line your mold of choice with a single banana leaf. Remove the leaves, lemongrass, and shallot from the rice, then use a spoon to pack the rice into the mold. It's best to complete this process while the rice is still warm so that the grains don't break or get mushed.

8 To serve, line a plate with a banana leaf. Flip the cone onto the plate and carefully ease out the rice. You can also add a small decorative crown of banana leaf or foil at the top.

9 Finally, surround the rice mountain with various **ACCOMPANYING DISHES.**

FRESH VEGETABLES
Cucumber and tomato slices

PHOTOGRAPHS BY MAREN CARUSO

OMELET

Use as many eggs as you would like. Javanese season their eggs with salt (1 pinch per egg) and sometimes finely chopped chives. Fry on both sides. Roll the omelet and cut into strips.

PERKEDEL KENTANG
POTATO PATTIES

Slice 3 potatoes into wedges, then fry until lightly browned. Finely chop 2 sprigs Chinese celery, 2 green onions, 2 garlic cloves, and 2 small shallots. Mash the potatoes with the chopped aromatics, salt, and white pepper. Shape into slider-sized patties and dip in 2 whisked eggs. Deep-fry.

SAMBAL KERING TEMPEH

Deep-fry ½ lb thinly sliced tempeh until golden brown. Set to drain on a paper napkin. In a food processor or blender, purée 1 small tomato, ½ teaspoon shrimp paste, a few fresh chilies (seeded if you like), 4 shallots, 4 garlic cloves, a pinch of sugar, and soy sauce. Dry-fry the paste over low heat for 10 minutes, then season to taste with salt and brown sugar. Add the tempeh and stir-fry for 3 more minutes.

ABON

Shredded and dried beef, available at Asian stores

WHAT WOULD DORIE DO?

with **DORIE GREENSPAN**

AS TOLD TO **RACHEL KHONG**

PORTRAIT BY WINNIE TRUONG

"HOLIDAYS AND BAKING ARE INEXTRICABLY BOUND, I AGREE WITH YOU," DORIE GREENSPAN IS TELLING ME. I NOD AFFIRMATIVELY, BUT THERE'S A DEEPER TRUTH SHE CAN'T ACKNOWLEDGE: THAT THE INEXTRICABLE BOND EXTENDS FROM HOLIDAYS AND BAKING TO DORIE GREENSPAN HERSELF. COME HOLIDAY SEASON, THE QUESTION ON THE MINDS OF LEGIONS OF BAKERS, MYSELF INCLUDED, IS: WHAT WOULD DORIE DO? THE LIKELIHOOD IS GREAT THAT DORIE HAS A RECIPE FOR WHATEVER YOU'RE LOOKING TO BAKE, WHETHER IT'S CHEESECAKE, RUGELACH, PUMPKIN PIE, OR GINGERBREAD. IT WILL BE FOOLPROOF AND ABSURDLY DELICIOUS; IT WILL SHAME ALL OTHER SWEETS AT THE POTLUCK TABLE.

Dorie (Greenspan is too formal a way to refer to her; when we tell friends where the recipe we've impressed them with is from, we say, "From Dorie") splits her time between Connecticut, New York, and Paris. "I'm an indiscriminate lover!" she says, about both where she's living and the holidays she celebrates. She's authored eleven cookbooks—including books with Daniel Boulud, Pierre Hermé, and Julia Child; her latest is *Baking Chez Moi*—but because her recipes are often accompanied by variations—a single Dorie recipe typically unfurls into several other recipes—it's really more like

she's written fifty cookbooks. Her writing is singular: suffused with enthusiasm and eagerness and a you've-got-to-try-this-ness that makes you want to bake all the things there are to bake and live all the lives there are to live.

"Baking is really special," she says. "We really don't just bake for ourselves. It's not like cooking, where you cook because you love to cook, or you cook because you have to cook. You bake to *share*. It's such a pleasure. Everything about it—from the ingredients to the way they feel and the way they combine. There are memories attached to baking, so I think that even the

scaredy-cats, the ones that don't have enough time, will bake for the holidays."

My family doesn't do big, intergenerational holidays; I've always been envious of families that do. Growing up, Dorie's didn't either. She taught herself to cook and bake only after marrying her husband, Michael, at age nineteen. Now they throw annual Thanksgiving feasts, Christmas dinners, and New Year's Eve get-togethers. Talking to Dorie, what occurs to me is that there are the things you choose, and those that choose you—the mix of all that is what makes a holiday, and a family, and a life. —RACHEL KHONG

I LIKED THE MAGIC

I didn't grow up with a holiday tradition. My mother didn't cook. My mother never baked, never ever ever. We didn't have big holiday meals.

I started cooking out of necessity. I was nineteen when I got married, and my parents were unhappy about my decision. There was a lot of, "This will never last." But I'm still married to the same guy. I met him when I was in high school and he was in college—he's four years older than I am. He left to go to graduate school at Stanford, and I was living in Brooklyn, so we wrote to each other. By the time he came back from graduate school, we knew each other so well. We hadn't actually dated, but we had four years of knowing each other as really good friends—we told each other everything.

I was married as a college student, and we had no money. Michael was working at a research center at Rockland State Hospital, doing biomedical research that I can't explain. We had this tiny little studio apartment with a closet that had been made into a kitchen. If we had an argument, one of us had to leave because there was no place to go. I was the first of all my friends to get married, to have my own apartment. It was like playing house. We had friends over to our place—the cubbyhole—three or four times a week. And I just loved it. I started cooking and baking because I had to, but I continued because I just loved having people around a table. I learned from books, and I still learn from books. Learning to bake was about playing to the crowd. I liked the magic of baking, having people say, *"You baked that?"*

THANKSGIVING

Michael had a completely different upbringing from mine. In some ways, I credit his mother and his family with making me want to cook and have people at the table. His parents both worked in Manhattan, in a showroom selling fancy kids' clothes, but Friday nights, they would always have a big dinner at home in Brooklyn. Their friends who worked nearby would come home with them. And dinner would just grow. It'd start out with six or eight people, and more people would come for dessert after they'd already had dinner. There'd be a whole second circle of people around the table.

My mother-in-law had five brothers, and her parents were bakers on the Lower East Side in the teens or early twenties. Every week, there was always a relative or brother at the table, and there would always be talk about, "Do you remember when Mom would make those rolls, and they'd still be warm, and we'd put a lot of butter on them?" Or, "Remember how, when Mom made meatballs, she would use the box grater to grate the garlic over it?" I had never, ever heard talk like this in my house. The memories themselves brought such joy, such happiness. I became a regular. I remember coming home one afternoon and seeing my mother-in-law working dough. I had never even touched dough!

Michael has great childhood memories, and both sides of his family were very close and saw one another a lot. There were best friends within the family; I didn't have that. For years, we didn't have our own holidays; we had theirs.

I remember the first year that I made Thanksgiving—how exciting it was and how nervous I was. I wanted it and I asked for it, and it was exciting to take it on. I made this string bean casserole that's still in my first notebook from when I got married. All of the recipes must have come from the back of boxes or something—it had sour cream, and a ton of swiss cheese, and cornflake crumbs.

I thought I was doing Michael's family a favor by hosting, but I think they felt differently. At their Thanksgiving, it was always traditional stuff. Thanksgiving was turkey and cranberry sauce out of a can. You'd open both ends of the can and tilt it out so you could see the lines of the can around it. The desserts would never be home-baked. There were cakes from Ebinger's, a famous Brooklyn bakery that made an amazing chocolate cake. My husband always remembers the huckleberry pie with crumbs on top. There were cookies from a bakery called Sutter's, also in the neighborhood. And there was fresh bread. There were *three* bakeries in close proximity. You got the bread from Ratchick's, you got the cake from Ebinger's, you got the cookies from Sutter's. And there wasn't much variation, whether it was a holiday or not.

My mother-in-law loves pumpkin pie. She's ninety-seven now, and every year, as soon as it's the season, I make pumpkin pie for her because she just loves it so much. I like to hear her say, "You make the *best* pumpkin pie." She always says, "Oh, I wasn't such a good cook. I didn't have time to cook." But she has a real feel for food, and she was the first person I saw really making something. The first rugelach I made, I made because of my mother-in-law. Her neighbor Ruth made it, and they taught me. They gave me the recipe on the little index card that goes in the green index card box.

CELEBRATE EVERYTHING

My family is Jewish, and so is Michael's. When we got married, we celebrated everything, and made the celebrations our own. There are so many holidays where there's something baked, so I celebrated everything. I colored Easter eggs. I frosted Easter candies. When Christmas came, I made tons of cookies. I had a Christmas tree one year that I decorated in gingerbread cookies, and it had very low-lying branches. A friend's kid came over and we found her on her back under the tree, nibbling the cookies. When our son was in school, I baked for the teachers.

I don't have "my traditional Christmas cake" or "what I make for the holiday," because I always want to be trying something new. I'm a very last-minute cook, which is why I'm always like, "What am I gonna do! What am I gonna do!" I try to plan a menu so I can go shopping, but then I get to the market and I see something else, and I'm happy to throw my menu away and start all over again.

For the past sixteen years we've celebrated Christmas and New Year's in Paris. It's pretty fabulous. For Christmas, I usually get a bûche de Noël from Pierre Hermé. I'll bake cookies, but I do nothing traditional. Paris is like New York. People come from all over, and when the holidays roll around, Paris isn't home for them. A lot of my younger French friends go home. People don't care about New Year's. I don't either, actually. I never went out for New Year's Eve, and so having people *in* was kind of my defense against ever having to go out. I could stay put and everybody could come to me.

Our table seats ten, but for New Year's Eve, we set up every inch of the apartment with tables and we do a sit-down dinner for whoever's around. We have our crew of regulars and whoever's in town and not away, and friends who are visiting from America. It's this funny little crowd—they range in age from thirty to seventysomething—and sometimes these people don't see one another all year, because they're my friends but not friends with each other. Last year, we were twenty-six. We always have oysters because they're great and they're fun and they look so wonderful when you put out big platters of them.

Right before midnight, we take bottles of champagne and glasses and we walk to the Pont des Arts, which is the bridge that connects the French Institute with the Louvre, over the Seine, and you can see the Eiffel Tower. We all go to the bridge at midnight. Everyone in Paris seems to be on the bridge. Sometimes there are fireworks. We toast the New Year. And then we come back to the apartment for dessert.

One year, we had so many people that we moved the party to a friend's restaurant that was closed for the holidays. We had a balthazar of champagne, which is like a piece of furniture. It's really huge. It took three guys to carry it out to the bridge. Everybody came back to the restaurant and said, "This is it! We're always going to have a balthazar. This is how you meet the best people." Out on the bridge, we poured for everybody. It was really, really fun.

I can't remember anything that I've cooked for New Year's. It always ends up being about the people and sharing the time with them.

I'VE BEEN SO LUCKY

People think I'm being naive when I say I've been so lucky. But I believe it. I stumbled into this. And I would not like to stumble out.

I was a secretary, I was a salesgirl, I was a substitute teacher. I went to graduate school and I worked at a research center. I didn't start working for a food magazine until I was in my thirties. I loved baking; I loved cooking; but I had no idea it could be a career. And it really wasn't, for women. My mother said to me, "If you were a nurse, people would know what you do." When I worked at the research center, I could never explain to people what I was doing. And the idea of food writing—that needed a subtitle, too.

My first baking job was at SoHo Charcuterie on Spring Street. I knew so little about food. I had never baked. I remember talking to someone, asking if I could get the job, and I said, "I bake every day, and

SPECULOOS

MAKES ABOUT 90 COOKIES

There are probably as many different recipes for speculoos as there are bakers, but all have cinnamon, brown sugar, and a fragrance that puts you in a Christmas mind-frame.

I shape these into logs and make slice-and-bake cookies, but you can roll them out and cut them with cookie cutters if you'd like. Since these are as good on their own as they are turned into a crumble, crust, or crumb, you might want to brush the logs with a beaten egg and roll them in sanding sugar before slicing and baking. In Belgium, where speculoos were born, the cookies celebrate Saint Nicolas and are, by definition, holiday treats. But if you love spice as much as I do, you'll make these year-round—deliciousness isn't seasonal.

All recipes reprinted with permission from the publisher Houghton Mifflin Harcourt, from Baking Chez Moi: Recipes from My Paris Home to Your Home Anywhere, *Copyright 2014.*

1 Whisk the flour, spices, and salt together in a medium bowl.

2 Working in the bowl of a stand mixer fitted with the paddle attachment, or in a large bowl with a hand mixer, beat the butter at medium speed until smooth, about 2 minutes. Add both sugars and the molasses and beat until the mixture is smooth again, about 3 minutes. Beat in the egg, and when it's incorporated, add the vanilla and mix for another 2 minutes. Add the dry ingredients all at once and pulse a few times to incorporate, then mix on low speed just until the flour disappears into the dough and the dough cleans the sides of the bowl.

3 Scrape the dough out onto a work surface and divide it into thirds. Using the palms of your hands, roll each piece of dough into an 8-inch-long log. Don't worry about the diameter: get the length right, and the diameter will be perfect. Wrap the logs tightly in plastic film and freeze for at least 3 hours.

4 When you're ready to bake: position the racks to divide the oven into thirds and preheat the oven to 375°F. Line three baking sheets with parchment paper or silicone baking mats.

5 Using a long, slender knife, slice off a sliver of dough from the end of one log to even it out, then cut the log into ¼-inch-thick rounds. Place them on one of the lined baking sheets and stow the sheet in the freezer while you cut the remaining logs. (The cookies hold their shape better if you bake them when they're cold.)

6 Bake the first two sheets of cookies for 11–13 minutes, rotating the sheets from top to bottom and front to back after 6 minutes, or until they are uniformly golden brown and almost firm at the center. Transfer the cookies to racks and cool to room temperature. Bake the third sheet of cookies.

7 Serving: speculoos are coffee's soul mate, but they're also really nice with tea and fine with mulled wine.

8 Storing: the logs of dough can be kept frozen for up to 2 months. There's no need to defrost them; just let them soften enough so that you can slice and bake them. Stored airtight, the baked cookies will keep at room temperature for up to 4 days.

▬ INGREDIENTS ▬

2 C all-purpose flour
1 T ground cinnamon
¾ t ground ginger
½ t freshly grated nutmeg
⅛ t ground cloves
½ t fine sea salt
1 stick (8 T) unsalted butter, at room temperature
½ C packed light brown sugar
¼ C sugar
2 T mild (light) molasses
1 large egg, at room temperature
1 t pure vanilla extract

I bake alone, and I want to talk to people about it, and I want to learn from other people, and I want to share ideas. No one I know wants to talk about baking!" The woman said to me, "Getting a job in a kitchen is not therapy. Perhaps you should go see someone." But I had this idea that it *would* be. Not therapy, but community.

I got fired. And then I went to work for Sarabeth Levine, who's still in business. She had just opened. My son Joshua was fifteen or eighteen months old. I was pushing him in my little stroller with a friend of mine who had a kid the same age. There was a sign on the door that said EXPERIENCED BAKER WANTED. My friend said to me, "That's for you!" Listen, I had one month's experience, and I was fired! She said, "You don't have to tell her that. Just go in and get that job." I said no, and she put my hands on her baby stroller and she said, "I'll be right back." She walked in and told Sarabeth that the baker she needed was outside and would show up the following morning. And I did.

I teasingly say I quit before I was fired. I never really got good. I never got fast. I never got good at production. I'm there saying, "Look at how pretty that is. Take a look. What if I put a little chocolate there?" Everyone else is saying, "We have to do 3,000 cookies..." It was a short-lived career. I'm glad that I'm just in my little kitchen. I love writing cookbooks. I know I will continue that. I like the idea that there are possibilities for something new. I just keep saying yes. Because you just don't know.

FAUX FRENCH

'm faux French, we know that—I'm Jewish, born in Brooklyn. But I fell in love with France and have stayed in love with France since. For a while I had this "If only my mother

had had me in Paris..." idea about life. I started asking chefs to teach me French food and baking so that I could make it mine. I could make a *galette des rois* for the holidays. I can make it and feel it's part of my tradition. I've been lucky enough to learn from these great chefs, and bold enough to play around with their recipes and turn them upside down.

When I was starting to work with Daniel Boulud on his cookbook, there was a fabulous French chef there who said, "Why are you doing this? Americans don't cook, and nobody follows recipes anyway." I was talking about how we were going to test the recipes, and he said, "Recipes are only inspiration." I thought maybe that's the difference between American and French home cooks, who've grown up knowing how to cook. But it didn't deter me from wanting to write recipes that were as functional as they were inspirational.

There's a recipe for a macaron in the cookbook I wrote with Pierre Hermé, and it runs, like, seven pages. It's endless. It's the macaron thesis. I struggled over it. The instructions were so detailed: open the oven, close the oven, stand upside down, whistle. I wanted people to succeed. And then I saw a recipe for macarons in French *Elle* that was a four-line caption. The whole recipe! And I thought, There's the difference.

I LOVE PIERRE!

I met Pierre Hermé in '91 or '92. I was doing a story for the *New York Times* on chestnuts, and I was in Paris, and chestnuts were used as decorations in store windows, they were everywhere. For the holidays, they make *marrons glacés*, which are these chestnuts soaked in syrup and wrapped in foil packets and sold for a fortune. I thought that would be a good recipe and I called Fauchon and said, "Could somebody please tell me

how you make marrons glacés?" They said, "The pastry chef is Pierre Hermé and I can't make an appointment for you; he has to call you." Pierre called and he said, "When would you like to come in?" And all I really wanted was for him to send me something. I went to meet Pierre and I took my husband because I thought this would be fifteen minutes and we would be out of there. Two hours later, we left kissing each other goodbye. And my husband says it was like he'd watched love happen. I fell in love with him and we kept in touch. He would call me when he came to New York, and I'd see him in Paris.

I was working on *Baking with Julia*, and the project was so intense, it was really heads down, just work, work, work, work, work. It was high anxiety, though not because of Julia, who was wonderful. When I finished it, I felt totally empty. Michael said, "And now you should write a book with Pierre Hermé." I said, "That's ridiculous." And he said, "No, write to him!"

That was the age of fax. I faxed Pierre and said, "This may sound like a crazy idea, but do you want to write a book together?" And he said, "I thought we already talked about this. Of course!"

So we worked together on the proposal. And then nothing. Nothing! I'd see him in Paris and we'd have dinner and I'd say, "Pierre, we have to work." He'd say, "I'm busy."

He'd call me, "How are things going?" And I'd say, "I'm getting a little nervous. We have a deadline." He'd say, "Don't worry, it'll all be okay!" Then he called and said, "I'm going on vacation." I said, "How nice."

He was married to Frédérick at the time. He said, "Frédérick and I are going on vacation. Why don't you come and we'll work?"

I said, "I think you and Frédérick should go on vacation."

"No, no, no, if you don't come, and we don't work on this, there isn't another moment."

OLIVE OIL AND WINE COOKIES

MAKES ABOUT 36 COOKIES

That these cookies are made with olive oil and wine is not surprising when you realize that they're a specialty of the Languedoc-Roussillon region in the South of France—it's one of the non-butter regions of the country and one known for its vast vineyards. But if the mix of oil and wine isn't surprising, just about every other thing about these cookies is: their shape is long, plump in the middle, and pointy at the ends, and they have a sophisticated flavor—first a little sweet, and then a little tangy, and finally, wonderfully mysterious. Right after they're baked, their texture is crunchy at the tips and cakey in the center—wait a day or so, and the chubby middle dries and starts to resemble a great tea biscuit. In fact, I like these best after they've had a little time to age and develop a crunchier texture and a more mellow flavor.

You can use any white wine or even any rosé you have on hand, but if you use a sweet or off-dry wine, you'll come closer to the original cookies, which are made with Muscat de Rivesaltes, a Roussillon star. In the Languedoc-Roussillon, these cookies are often flavored with orange-flower water (instead of vanilla, which was my idea) or enriched with anise seeds. My favorite addition is grated orange (or tangerine or clementine) zest. To get the most out of the zest, first put the sugar in the mixing bowl, sprinkle over the zest, and use your fingers to rub the sugar and zest together until the sugar is moist and aromatic. Add the rest of the dry ingredients and continue with the recipe.

1 Position the racks to divide the oven into thirds and preheat the oven to 350°F. Line two baking sheets with parchment paper or silicone baking mats.

2 Whisk the flour, sugar, baking powder, and salt together in a large bowl. Pour in the olive oil, switch to a flexible spatula, and stir to incorporate—you don't have to be thorough now. Stir the vanilla extract into the wine, then pour the wine mixture into the bowl and mix until you have an easy-to-work-with dough. It will be smooth on the outside, but peek inside and you'll see that it looks like a sponge; when you pinch and pull it, you'll be surprised at how stretchy it is.

3 Divide the dough into pieces about the size of a large cherry or small walnut and roll each one into a ball. Next, roll each ball under your palm to shape it into a short sausage. When you've got the sausage shape, press down on the ends with your thumb and pinkie (don't press the center), and roll up and back a few times to form a cookie about 4 inches long that is just a little plump in the center and tapered at the ends. Dredge each cookie in sugar and arrange the cookies on the baking sheets. (Before they're dredged, the shaped cookies can be frozen on the lined baking sheets, and then, when firm, packed airtight and kept in the freezer for up to 2 months. There's no need to defrost before baking.)

4 Bake the cookies for 20–22 minutes, rotating the baking sheets

INGREDIENTS

- **2¾ C** all-purpose flour
- **½ C** sugar, plus more for dredging
- **½ t** baking powder
- **¼ t** fine sea salt
- **½ C** olive oil, extra-virgin or not, preferably fruity
- **½ t** pure vanilla extract
- **½ C** white wine, preferably sweet (see headnote)

from top to bottom and front to back after 10 minutes, until the cookies have brown tips and bottoms and golden bellies. (If baking from frozen, dredge the cookies in sugar and bake a minute or two longer.) Cool the cookies on the baking sheets and, if you can stand it, wait at least a day before serving.

5 Serving: this is the kind of cookie that might come to a French table as the go-along with a fruit salad, but they're also great with coffee or tea—their shape and texture just about call out "Dunk, dunk." Although it's not at all traditional, I serve them with white wine in the summer. They're sweeter than the usual aperitif cracker, but they're much more surprising.

6 Storing: of course you can serve these cookies as soon as they reach room temperature, but I think they're better a couple of days later. Packed into a container, they will keep at room temperature for at least 5 days.

So I said, "Okay if I bring Michael?"

"Oh, sure."

The four of us lived for a week in a small beach cottage, and every morning, Pierre would go to the market and come back with newspapers and croissants and coffee. He would roll up this table with electrical cords, plug it in the cottage, and roll it down to the beach, and we'd have four laptops on the table. Everyone who sailed by thought it was so peculiar. We had a generator for a lamp when we worked late. Pierre brought milk crates with recipes in them, and we sat on the beach and went through the recipes. I would read through them and have questions. I assumed that Pierre and I would bake together, but there wasn't time for that. It was an amazing week. We would work all morning. Then we would go to the market late in the morning and buy stuff and cook lunch. Then we would plug in again and work until we had to stop for dinner. Then we would plug in again and work until midnight.

I went home to New York with this stack of recipes. I would bake them and freeze the results, and when Pierre came to New York, he would taste everything and work in the kitchen with me on stuff I had trouble with. When I would go to Paris, I would bring him stuff and we would talk some more. It was a very long-distance project. I'd fly to Paris on a Thursday night, and Pierre and I would work all weekend, and I would fly back. It was because of that book that we first started thinking about an apartment in Paris.

Pierre is so smart. He's so crazy creative. And he's very quiet. Really, really quiet. He's quiet with a twinkle. When something makes him happy, you see it—it's all in his eyes. He never knew where something was going to come from. He always had a notebook, and he's crazy about music, he reads a lot, he's interested in art. He's always taking little notes that might become something. I've never met anybody with the same sort of flavor combinations, that sense of what can go together.

All great chefs have it, but there's something that Pierre does that's different. A lot of things come from aroma, come from fragrance. Certainly *ispahan*, the rose dessert that he does. It's rose, lychee, and raspberry. He had tried to do a rose dessert in the late eighties and no one was interested. But he held that idea and kept working with it and kept playing with it. The ispahan was originally just rose macarons with rose cream, and now there are like fifteen things that are based on the trinity he ultimately arrived at: rose, lychee, and raspberry.

I always hold that up as an ideal of creativity. How you can take one idea and keep working on it, and see the possibilities, to go deeper and deeper and deeper and wider and wider and wider on something, and how the flavors change with texture. He's still working with those flavors. He did a book all on ispahan. I took a picture a couple years ago in the supermarket. There's a yogurt that was rose, lychee, and raspberry. That trinity has gone everywhere. You see it all over France. You can go to the tiniest little village and somebody's making a rose macaron.

I learned so much from him about flavor, but also about how to work, how to create, his insistence on quality. He's had people who've worked for him ever since he started. People love working with him, and I think that's marvelous. And he's funny and encouraging and such a good teacher and a really good friend. I love Pierre!

For Christmas, he does several bûches de Noël. He'll make an ispahan bûche de Noël, or he has this chocolate creation that I love that has chunks of chocolate and salt crystals in it. It's normally a cake, but that will become a bûche de Noël. They're always beautiful. They're always sleek, modern, sophisticated. Pierre doesn't do decoration. You don't put something there just for color; it has to be part of the dessert. I remember going out to eat to dinner with him, and we were served ice cream with a mint leaf on it, and he took the mint leaf and threw it across the table. Pierre's desserts are almost plain-looking—everything is there for taste or texture. They look beautiful, but that's not the first consideration.

MORE THAN I TRUST MYSELF

I had dinner with Pierre the last time we were in Paris, and I said to him, "You trust me more than *I* trust me." I know a few people in my life who are like that. My agent, my husband, my son Joshua, and Pierre—they're always sure that I can do what I'm not sure I can do. They trust me more than I trust myself.

Michael was the one who said, "Don't go back to your old job. Try to be a baker." He's always been the one to say, "Try it." He's always been incredibly encouraging.

Michael teasingly says—I think it's probably true—he became an engineer because there was no language requirement, and he couldn't imagine that he would ever need a foreign language, and certainly, it wouldn't be French. And now he's living in Paris. I think we both made each other. We were kids. It sounds like a cliché to say we grew up together, but we became who we are together and because of each other.

And Michael has always kind of known ahead of time what I should do.

I get scared. I mean, look at my posture. In my next life, when I'm five-foot-ten and blond, I'll forge ahead, but lots of things scare me. *Most* things scare me. But it's the excitement of trying something new that overcomes the fear. And there's Michael, who says, "Go." LP

MERVEILLES

MAKES ABOUT 40 PASTRIES

Merveille means "miracle," and the name is not hyperbole. Can sweet, brandied egg dough, fried until puffed and then sugared until it poses a threat to shirt-fronts, be anything less than a miracle? The pastry, a centuries-old sweet from France's Aquitaine, the region that claims Bordeaux as its capital, was traditionally made for Carnival, but knowing a good thing when they see it, the Aquitains now make it throughout the year.

In Provence, a similar dough is cut into squares and called *oreillers,* or "pillows," and in Lot, in the southwest, the dough is cut into bands, sandwiched, and twisted. I've seen trapezoidal merveilles and pastries shaped into rings. Depending on the location, the recipe might or might not include yeast (I use baking powder); the fat for frying might be olive oil, goose fat, shortening, or grapeseed or canola oil; and the spirit that flavors it might be rum, eau-de-vie, Armagnac, or whatever is local.

With so much variety in their homeland, merveilles are yours to do with as you want. I usually cut the dough into long strips or small triangles with a fluted ravioli wheel. My oil of choice is canola or grapeseed, and my moment of choice is anytime there are a lot of people around. This is a party sweet, and one that's the most fun—and the messiest—to eat when the dough is just shy of too hot.

1 Whisk the flour, baking powder, and salt together in a small bowl.

2 Put the sugar in a medium bowl and sprinkle the orange zest over it. Using your fingertips, rub the sugar and zest together until the sugar is moist and fragrant. Toss the butter into the bowl and work it into the sugar with a sturdy flexible spatula. Pour in the egg, brandy or rum, and vanilla, and stir to blend as best as you can. At this point, the mixture will look like egg drop soup—don't be discouraged. Add the dry ingredients and stir until the dough, which will be soft and moist and very much like a sticky muffin dough, comes together.

3 Turn out the dough, wrap it in plastic film, and chill it for at least 2 hours. (The dough can be refrigerated for as long as overnight.)

4 When you're ready to roll and cut the dough, line a baking sheet with plastic film.

5 Cut the dough in half and return one half to the refrigerator. Flour your work surface well—this is a sticky dough and will need more flour than you might usually use—and flour the top of the dough. Roll it out, turning it over to make sure it's not sticking, rolling on both sides and adding more flour if necessary. Once the surface is properly floured and you've got the dough going, it's very easy to roll, and you'll be able to roll it until it's paper-thin, which is what you want. If you can roll it into a large rectangle, great; if it's more free-form, that's fine, too.

6 Working with a fluted pastry wheel, ravioli cutter, plain pizza wheel, or a knife, cut the dough into long strips, squares, diamonds,

or any other shape that appeals to you. (I go for strips that are about 1 inch wide and 3 inches long; for more drama, you can go longer.) Place the strips on the lined baking sheet and cover with another piece of plastic film. Repeat with the remaining dough, cover with the plastic, and chill for at least 1 hour.

7 When you're ready to fry: have a baking sheet lined with a triple thickness of paper towels near the stove. Have a skimmer, tongs, or chopsticks (my favorite tool here) on hand as well. Fill a sugar duster or strainer (or two) with cinnamon sugar and/or confectioners' sugar. Pour 4 inches of oil into a large, deep saucepan (or use an electric deep fryer) and heat it to 350°F, as measured on a deep-fat thermometer.

8 Drop 4–6 merveilles into the pan—don't crowd them—and fry until they're golden on both sides, 2–3 minutes. Lift them out of the oil with the skimmer or other tool, allowing the excess oil to drip back into the pan, then turn out onto the paper towel–lined baking sheet to drain. Pat the tops with more paper towels to remove surface oil, then dust both sides with sugar(s) while the cookies are still hot and slightly moist from the oil. Continue frying the remaining merveilles—making sure to keep the oil at 350°F—draining, patting dry, and dusting until all the dough is fried.

9 Serving: these are best eaten as soon as they're cool enough to bite into, but they're also delicious at room temperature. If the sugar has melted into the cookies, dust them again before serving.

10 Storing: these are not really keepers, and that's not a bad thing because it's unlikely that you'll have any left to keep. However, if there are a few, you can keep them overnight in a dry place; don't refrigerate.

INGREDIENTS

1 C all-purpose flour
½ t baking powder
¼ t fine sea salt
3 T sugar
+ grated zest of 1 orange
1 T unsalted butter, at room temperature
1 large egg, lightly beaten, at room temperature
2 T brandy or dark rum
1 t pure vanilla extract
+ cinnamon sugar and/or confectioners' sugar, for dusting
+ flavorless oil, such as grapeseed or canola, for deep-frying

GINGERBREAD BÛCHE DE NOËL

MAKES 12 SERVINGS

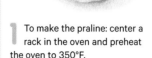

Yule logs are such a part of the French Christmas tradition that a month or two before the holiday, *pâtisseries* start previewing their new creations, rather like fashion designers with their collections. And weeks before, every newspaper and food magazine runs a photo-filled story on what the top pastry houses will offer. It's a dream book and a shopping list rolled into one.

Since we spend the holidays in Paris, I get a chance to sample a few cakes each season. My bûche strategy for dinners at home is simple: one time I'll buy one, the next time I'll bake one. With so many fanciful cakes in the shops, making my own is unnecessary, but I'll never give it up, mostly because it's so much fun to make a rolled-up cake and even more fun to serve it. It's a project, yes, but a completely satisfying and delicious one.

This bûche has the flavor of gingerbread—it's spiced with cinnamon, ginger, and black pepper, sweetened with brown sugar, and rolled up around a cream cheese and praline filling that's lick-the-spoon wonderful. (The filling, packed in a jar, is a great gift on its own, to be spread over toast or on cookies.) The pecan praline is quick and easy to make, and it adds terrific flavor and crunch. I chop some of it very finely—you can crush it, if you prefer—and stir it into the filling. I chop the remainder a little more coarsely and sprinkle it over the billowing, snow-white marshmallow frosting. Everything but the frosting can be made ahead, so you can get a jump on things. You need to spread the frosting as soon as it's made, but the cake needs to be refrigerated after it's filled and it can stay in the fridge for up to 2 days, so there are no last-minute to-dos with this beauty.

And just because it's called a bûche de Noël doesn't mean you can't stud it with candles and call it a birthday cake.

A word on tools: you'll need a candy thermometer, a pastry brush, a stand mixer or hand mixer, and a ruler.

1 To make the praline: center a rack in the oven and preheat the oven to 350°F.

2 Line a baking sheet with parchment or a silicone baking mat and spread the pecans out on top. Bake the nuts for 3 minutes (you want to heat them, not toast them), stir them around, and then put them in a warm spot while you cook the sugar.

3 Put the sugar in a small saucepan and pour in the water. Swirl to moisten the sugar, then put the pan over medium-high heat. Cook the sugar, washing down the sides of the pan if needed with a pastry brush dipped in cold water, until the sugar turns a medium amber color. (Stay close; sugar changes color quickly.) Turn off the heat, add the nuts to the saucepan (set the lined baking sheet aside), and stir a few times with a heat-proof spatula or a wooden spoon, just to coat the nuts with syrup. Pour the caramelized nuts back out onto the lined baking sheet and use the spatula, spoon, or an offset metal spatula to spread them out. If they won't spread out, no matter—you're going to chop them anyway. Let cool completely. (The praline can be made up to a day ahead, packed in a container, and kept in a cool, dry place—moisture is praline's nemesis.) Finely chop ½ cup of the praline; coarsely chop the remainder.

4 To make the cake: center a rack in the oven and preheat the oven to 350°F. Line a 12-by-17-inch rimmed baking sheet

with a piece of parchment paper. Butter the paper, dust with flour, and tap out the excess.

5 Whisk the flour, cornstarch, cinnamon, ginger, salt, and pepper together in a small bowl.

6 Have a wide skillet about one-third full of simmering water

— INGREDIENTS —

FOR THE PRALINE
1 C pecan halves or pieces
⅓ C sugar
¼ C water

FOR THE CAKE
+ unsalted butter, softened, for buttering the pan
¾ C all-purpose flour (+ more for dusting the pan)
¼ C cornstarch, sifted
¾ t ground cinnamon
¾ t ground ginger
¼ t fine sea salt
¼ t freshly ground black pepper
6 large eggs
¾ C packed light brown sugar
½ stick (4 T) unsalted butter, melted and cooled
+ confectioners' sugar, for dusting and rolling

FOR THE FILLING
8 oz cream cheese, at room temperature
1 stick (8 T) unsalted butter, at room temperature
Pinch fine sea salt
½ t ground cinnamon
2 t pure vanilla extract

FOR THE FROSTING
½ C egg whites (about 4 large)
1 C sugar
¾ t cream of tartar
1 C water
1 T pure vanilla extract

on the stove. Working in the bowl of a stand mixer or in a heat-proof bowl in which you can use a hand mixer, whisk together the eggs and brown sugar. Set the bowl in the pan of simmering water (pour off some water if you're concerned that it will slosh over the sides) and whisk nonstop until the mixture is very warm to the touch but not set, about 2 minutes. Remove from the heat.

7 If you're using a stand mixer, attach the bowl to the stand and fit it with the whisk attachment, or use a hand mixer. Working on high speed, beat the sugared eggs until they are thick and pale, have more than doubled in volume, and have reached room temperature, 7–10 minutes. Switch to a flexible spatula and fold in the flour mixture in 2 additions. Be as delicate as you can and don't be overly thorough now—you're going to continue to fold when the butter goes in. Put the melted butter in a small bowl, scoop a big spoonful of the batter over it, and stir. Turn this mixture out onto the batter in the bowl and fold it in: cut deep into the center of the bowl and search the bottom for unincorporated flour—find it and fold it in. Scrape the batter out onto the prepared baking sheet and spread it evenly with an offset spatula.

8 Bake for 13–15 minutes, or until the cake is golden brown, lightly springy to the touch, and starting to pull away from the sides of the baking sheet. Transfer the baking sheet to a cooling rack, but keep it on the rack for no more than 5 minutes; you want to roll the cake while it's hot.

9 Lay a cotton or linen kitchen towel (not terrycloth or microfiber) on the counter and dust it generously with confectioners' sugar. Run a table knife around the sides of the cake and invert the cake onto the towel. Carefully peel away the parchment. Lightly dust the cake with confectioners'

sugar and replace the parchment, putting the clean side against the cake (or use a new piece). Starting at a short end, roll the cake into a log; this is a pre-roll, so it doesn't have to be tight or perfect. If the cake cracks, keep rolling—the filling and frosting will patch everything. Return the rolled-up cake (still in its towel) to the rack and let it cool, seam side down, to room temperature.

10 Meanwhile, make the filling: put the softened cream cheese, butter, and salt in the bowl of a stand mixer fitted with the paddle attachment, or work in a large bowl with a hand mixer. With the mixer on medium speed, beat until the cream cheese and butter are homogeneous and smooth. Beat in the cinnamon and vanilla. If you're going to use the filling now, stir in the ½ cup finely chopped praline; if not, wait until you're ready to fill the Yule log. Transfer to a bowl, cover, and refrigerate. (You can make the filling—without the praline—up to 2 days ahead and keep it well covered in the refrigerator.)

11 To fill the log: if the filling has been chilled, give it a good whisking to return it to a spreadable consistency; add the praline if you haven't already done so. Unroll the log and carefully remove the parchment; leave the cake on the kitchen towel. Beginning with a short end, gently roll up the cake, peeling away the towel as you go. Unroll the cake onto the towel or a clean piece of parchment.

12 Spread the filling across the surface of the cake, leaving a scant 1-inch border uncovered on the long sides. Again, starting from a short side, roll up the cake, leaving the towel or parchment behind and trying to get as tight a roll as you can. If you like, tighten the log using the paper-and-ruler technique.* Place the cake on a parchment-lined cutting board, cover it, and chill it for 30 minutes.

13 Meanwhile, make the frosting: put the egg whites in the clean, dry bowl of a stand mixer fitted with the whisk attachment or in a large bowl that you can use with a hand mixer. Stir the sugar, cream of tartar, and water together in a small saucepan. Bring to a boil over medium-high heat, then cover and boil for about 3 minutes. Uncover, attach a candy thermometer to the pan, and cook until the thermometer reads 242°F (this can take almost 10 minutes).

14 When the sugar reaches 235°F, begin beating the whites on medium speed. If you get to the point where the whites look like they're about to form stiff peaks and the syrup isn't at 242°F yet, lower the mixer speed and keep mixing until the sugar is ready.

15 At 242°F, with the mixer on medium speed, stand back and carefully and steadily pour the hot syrup into the bowl. Try to get the syrup between the side of the bowl and the whisk. Perfection is impossible, so ignore any spatters; don't try to stir them into the frosting. Add the vanilla and keep beating until the frosting cools to room temperature, about 5 minutes. You'll have a shiny marshmallow frosting, which you should spread now.

16 To frost and finish the log: remove the cake from the refrigerator. You can frost it on the cutting board and then transfer it to a serving platter or put it on the platter now. To keep the platter clean during frosting, tuck strips of parchment under the log, putting just a sliver of the parchment under the cake and leaving the lion's share to protect your platter.

17 If the ends of the log look ragged, trim them. Using an offset spatula, table knife, or the back of a spoon, swirl the frosting all over the cake in a thick layer. Refrigerate for at least 1 hour

to set the frosting. Sprinkle the cake with the remaining coarsely chopped praline before serving.

18 Serving: bringing the cake to the table is its own dramatic event, but there's no reason not to add to the drama by making it the sole event. Instead of waiting to serve the log après dinner, have an afternoon holiday party and serve just the cake and champagne. It's a very chic way to say Merry Christmas!

19 Storing: covered lightly and kept away from foods with strong odors, the cake will keep in the refrigerator for up to 2 days. Serve it chilled.

* When you're making logs of cookie dough or rolling up a bûche de Noël, you want to get logs that are as tight as possible and, particularly in the case of cookies, free of air pockets. (It's the pockets that give you holes in your cookies.) To tighten your logs, you'll need a ruler and a large sheet of parchment (my choice) or wax paper. With a short edge of the paper toward you on the counter, place the cookie or cake log horizontally on the paper about one third up from the edge closest to you. Fold the top portion of the paper all the way over the log.

Grab the ruler with one hand and grab the part of the parchment that's closest to you (the bottom part) with the other. Wedge the ruler against the bottom of the log (on top of the folded-over parchment). Push the ruler under the log at the same time that you pull the bottom paper toward you. Don't be afraid to put a little muscle into the pulling and pushing; it will help you get a firm log. If your log is longer than your ruler, move the ruler along the log to ensure that it's uniformly compact.

Lift the paper off the dough and admire your work—for all the years that I've been doing this, I still think of it as a neat party trick.

BRING YOUR DAUGHTER TO WORK DAY

BY JULIA COOKE

NANA'S HOUSE IN WESTCHESTER, EASTER DINNER: LOUD, HEAVY WOMEN ORBITING THE STOVE.

As a small child, I was left to play with my sister or bother the men in the living room while my mother, her mother, and her sisters cooked. We sat in the dining room, which never got much light, at the broad, long table, surrounded by velvety fleur-de-lis wallpaper. My Aunt Bia (I couldn't say "Maria") twisted hip-first through the creaky swinging door between the kitchen and dining room with a platter of nutty-smelling meat. My favorite was something called sweetbreads. I liked the name.

The first time I remember thinking my mother's work as a food writer made my life different was when she made spaghetti with meatballs three nights in a row, trying to get the proportions perfect for a recipe. I was around eleven years old. Tuesday's meat mix was fattier, the spice blend on Wednesday less pungent. But there were leftovers from Tuesday when she began cooking on Wednesday. Stacks of Tupperware filled with leftovers made a Tetris game out of visiting the refrigerator.

By Thursday the recipe was perfected, and on Friday I pressed my cheek to the cool Formica of the kitchen counter and swore I'd vomit if I had to eat more meatballs. We were rarely offered alternate dinners—pickiness was not an option—but by the third night of spaghetti, my sister and I were allowed to forage in the fridge and make what we wanted.

My family ate dinner together at least six nights of every week, always at the dining room table, no TV, and each of us had to contribute to putting the meal on the table. This did not seem strange to me until I was a teenager, when I discovered that none of my friends ate with their families between all of the practices, meetings, homework, and dances. Meanwhile, we sliced cucumber for the salad or set the table, did the dishes or put the fish under the broiler, and dipped the rice paper for Vietnamese salad rolls in warm water—carefully, so they didn't tear.

I was twelve when I saw a calf carcass for the first time, in the window at Biancardi Meats on Arthur Avenue. We had recently moved from New York to Oregon and were back for a visit. My mom had taken Nana, my sister, and me to the Bronx. She wanted us to know where our traditions came from, to see the last vestige of visibly Italian New York and understand the steaming plates of meat we ate on Easter, to see stores that bore signs that looked like my mother's last name: Biancardi, Madonia, Randazzo. I hadn't known before where sweetbreads came from. It was the pancreas, Nana told me, as she held my hand in front of the butcher's window, and I swore off meat. (My vegetarianism lasted two years. I ordered a hamburger one day when I was fourteen and that was that.)

ILLUSTRATIONS BY ELENI KALORKOTI

Everything about my family felt demanding: we had more rules, we didn't watch much TV, we rarely ate the straightforward kinds of dinners my friends ate. My mother would call me downstairs to help, and I'd stand sullenly next to the sink to chop vegetables for the salad we always ate with dinner. The rhythm of the knife—guillotining the carrots, then the cucumbers, now chopping the tomatoes—hypnotized me. Lost in the trance of kitchen activity, I wouldn't realize I'd begun to answer my mother's questions: how was school, what movie did I see with Nicole last weekend, did I like *The Things They Carried*?

She says that she felt like she got her daughter back for those fifteen

searching for the chef. When the food came, she would poke at it too long with her fork. Her eyes would glint when she realized what was happening inside a dish—when she could deconstruct a meal—or when it was so good, so complex, that she couldn't.

She took photos, too. The practice was even more obtrusive before the smartphone, when my mother would pull an enormous camera out of her purse at dinner, wave her hands with an admonishment not to start on our meals yet, twist the plate around until it was in the best position, and sometimes stand in front of her chair, trying to get just enough distance to light the food well. We'd pass our plates along. I'd sense other patrons

24th. We press the dough into balls first and then push our weight onto rolling pins, one shoulder higher than the other for leverage, to flatten them. After a decade, we still tear the too-thin parts. We spread the sautéed scallions with olives and anchovies onto the once-baked bottom crust in the broad baking pan, and place the other half of the dough on top. My mother and father always stand by to watch this last step, tentative like a game of Jenga in a late round: each of us picks up one side of the layer and sets it on top of the slimy green pie, then crimps the edges against the pan.

My dad, in his role as sous chef, boils and cuts all the seafood for the salad, and then my mother pours in

minutes every night. I felt differently.

I resented eating the same dish over and over when my mom was on deadline. Ricotta cheesecake for days, those salad rolls, frittatas. If we had demands, they'd wait. My teenage memories place my mother hovering over the stove with her notepad, waving her hand in the steam to pull it toward her flared nostrils, her forehead creased. When she brought me to a good restaurant, what was on the plate often captivated her more than what I said. I would get what felt like twenty or so minutes—of a ninety-minute meal—of my mother's full attention. The rest of the time, she looked through the window of the open kitchen into the sizzle and pop,

glancing over and boil inside with the sense that my mother's profession robbed food of its fun.

The spectacle of Christmas Eve dinner with my family begins every year around the 17th of December. My mother calls seafood providers to compare prices and place our orders: squid, shrimp, scallops, conch for seafood salad, clams, and lobster. Salt cod sometimes, too, if we're ambitious. It's the Feast of the Seven Fishes. My father picks everything up, my mother makes sure we have all of the other ingredients on the 23rd (produce, anchovies, pasta, prosecco), and my sister Lizzy and I, now well into adulthood, make the scallion pie on the morning of the

lemon juice and oil and garlic powder and chopped parsley, because only she knows the correct proportions. Lizzy makes tiramisu for dessert, soaking the ladyfingers in espresso and eating the ones that break. She vibrates by the time it's done. We listen to Christmas carols on the radio and dance. The linguine with clam sauce is the easiest and the recipe I love most, because it can feed a crowd; I serve it to friends throughout the year.

There is yelling; the day progresses slower than we've planned. My sister disappears upstairs to make a phone call and I check my e-mail, and my mother says that we expect her to do everything and it's just *so typical* and next year we shouldn't do it at all;

we'll eat turkey or a rack of lamb like everyone else, the Italian thing is too much of a production. It sometimes feels like we can't possibly meet her enormous expectations—that short of acquiring clogs and whites, neither the food nor the day will be quite good enough. Even so, it's one of my favorite days of the year.

My mother was not circumscribed by her Italianness—by Catholicism and nuns at school and men named Vincent and the food of her youth. Where my mother was intellectually curious, her family was dogmatic. During the sixties and seventies, she pulled for independence, for universality, as they got more insular. My mother was the smartest of her sisters: introspective, analytical, ambitious. She traveled, became a journalist, took the assignments that were usually given to the men in the newsroom, married a liberal Irish American. It wasn't until later that she began to write about food. I'm older now than my mother was when she married my father, in the wedding that my mother's dad initially said he wouldn't pay for—they had lived together before the engagement.

We'd notice as we got older, my sister and I, that whenever we went as a family to visit my grandmother, my mother would shrink. Her shoulders tightened, her mouth took on a brittleness—nothing like the supple smiles she wore at home, or the tightly wound frowns we knew signaled her frustration. At least at home her expressions varied. When in college I visited her family alone, my aunts would speak derisively of my mother, one-off barbs spoken without looking in my eyes, throwaways that I could easily ignore. *You know how she is.* There was something needy and mean in my aunts, as if the only way they knew to get closer to me or my sister was to cut our mother down. When the comments turned more aggressive, I'd shrug and say I loved my mother, and sure, she was critical and sometimes

too clingy, but she was still my mother, and she was funny and warm and giving, too. As I got older, my respect for my mother became a wall—something I constructed to keep her family out.

Food, I saw, was the place where my mother could enjoy her family's company even when she didn't, where family stories could be told sans fraught emotional outbursts. My mother could take the thing she was happy to inherit from them and spin it into something that gave her independence and identity, into an endeavor in which her perfectionism and worldliness paid off. She is generous with her passion for food—she will take time to ruminate when I call from a supermarket across the country to ask if the clam sauce might be good with crushed tomatoes and arugula and pork sausage, like the cookbook she gave me for Christmas suggested. But though we share some of her weekly excitements for tagines, Himalayan salt blocks, or drinking vinegars, the drive belongs to her. I have never invented or tried, time after time, to perfect a recipe.

My sister and I have promised to produce this year's Christmas Eve meal ourselves, from the phone calls and the pickups, to cooking and stabbing the lobsters, with which, realistically, we will ask my father's help.

When I was four, I insisted on walking down the streets of New York a half-block in front of my mother. We'd get off the subway, emerge into the light from the clatter underground, and I'd rush ahead and shout that she should stay behind me. Maybe what I share most with my mother is a terse desire for both independence and family. For a time, when I was in my early twenties, she was taken with the notion that I would be a food writer, too. "You were raised with a palate," she sighed after a few glasses of wine—after I'd correctly identified the spices in a Peruvian dish. But what my mother's job gave me was not a calling of my own. Rather, she enabled me

to cook my way through failure and rejection, buoyed by a sense of my own competence. Heartbroken at twenty-four, I kept my friends' pantries stocked with scones and made pasta dinners three times weekly. Cooking stews gets me through writing drafts, the tangible contrasting with the abstraction of migrant colons and paragraphs. My boyfriend makes fun of how aggrieved I still look when my mother asks interminable questions of restaurant waitstaff and chefs, but I'm trying not to complain as much.

I took a series of photographs of my mother on a family vacation we took to Vietnam, the year we decided we wouldn't do Italian Christmas or gifts. We ate streetside pho and lemongrass fish in Hanoi; got sick at the tourist-trap restaurant run by a deaf man and his eight eager children in Hue; and finally, in Saigon, found the famous pho hall my mother had been talking about the whole time.

They serve big, steaming bowls of rich beef broth and noodles, leave a bucket of herbs and greens on the table for you to add to the soup as you like, and bring a tray of things that look like churros to dip. You have the option of three different chili sauces in plastic squeeze bottles. The tables are all communal; aluminum chair legs clink together as patrons come and go. My mother wanted to try all of the wrapped pastries, but only a bite of each. She'd unwrap one, smell it, taste it, nod, and hand it absentmindedly to either my sister, me, or my father, at which point Lizzy would laugh, I would groan, and my father would shrug. There was one that was gummy, wrapped in banana leaves, and filled with something resembling bean paste. I took six photos in immediate succession: Mom looking confusedly down at the little packet in her hand, holding it up to her nose, taking a bite, chewing slowly, and smiling, bashful but radiant. The final frame shows her reaching out, with the banana-leaf packet in her hand, toward me. **LP**

THE
WARNING
SHIFT

BY **LEE ELLIS**

ILLUSTRATIONS BY MICHAEL TUNK

LIKE THE OTHER SIX OR EIGHT HOOTERS I'VE BEEN TO, INCLUDING ONE IN SWITZERLAND WHERE, IN A EUROPEAN REVERSAL, THE SERVERS DRESSED MORE PURITANICALLY THAN THEIR AMERICAN COUNTERPARTS, THE AMARILLO CHAPTER HAS BEEN SCRUBBED RAW, AND A FUME OF CITRUS DISINFECTANT HANGS HEAVY IN THE AIR UNTIL THE MOMENT THEY PUT FOOD BEFORE YOU. FLAT-PANEL TELEVISIONS, BOLTED TO THE WALLS AND BEAMS, SHOW EITHER SPORTS OR SPORTS ANALYSIS. MUSIC PLAYS LOUDLY: POWER BALLADS, JIMMY BUFFETT, SONGS JIMMY BUFFETT MIGHT LISTEN TO. THIS IS THE EXTENT OF THE AMARILLO HOOTERS' DAZZLE AND IT'S FINE. I'M FINE WITH IT. INSIDE YOU DON'T FEEL SO BAD THINKING YOUR ANIMAL THOUGHTS, THE ONES ABOUT EATING AND THE BODY, AND THEY KEEP IT COOL IN HERE, ALMOST CHILLY, WHILE OUTSIDE A TEXAS SUN WITH NO CLOUDS TO FILTER IT PRESENTS THE WORLD BLUNTLY.

I am given two servers. The first has no opinion on the Cadillac Ranch, my destination for later this afternoon, and the second, who takes over during the dinner switch, thinks the Ranch can be seen pretty good from the interstate, doing eighty. When I mention that it ranks very high on lists of Amarillo attractions, the second server makes a noise. "Probably Hooters does too," she says.

Still, I want my picture of the Ranch. A tourist's picture, evidence of a visit. I want to see something in the Texas Panhandle that I can say I've seen. Otherwise, there's going to be a hole in this little cross-country quest not far from the start, here at

the edge of the West. Only a week after Labor Day, when the trip got underway, it's early yet to be missing the regional wonders.

Labor Day and, without employment, I set off in a leased faux SUV, dainty and practical, to cross the American interior with hope of a job on the other side. The work, I'm told, is seasonal black-market labor conducted in an Upper California backwater, a place that my employer says can't be named on the phone. I'm to drive to a town on the Pacific coast and call him for further instructions. What few details he offers about the job that may or may not be waiting for me there are hidden in a slang he knows I don't know, a cryptic insider's dialect designed, it seems, to appeal to the outsider. Yesterday this employer told me to turn around, that the thing we'd been talking about was off, but I didn't. Today it's back on and the westering continues.

At the time of my departure, the significance of it being Labor Day didn't register, as the holiday, like so many holidays, isn't really a holiday when one isn't employed. It's Monday, September something. Now, though, I'm a week nearer work, thirteen-hundred-plus miles from my origin point, and there's a squat wooden bowl of curly fries on the table. Journey crashes in the background. The fries, compared to other fries found in the many sacks of road food I've eaten this trip, mark a high point. How many taste tests has Hooters conducted to reach this fry?

My bowl nearly empty, I turn back to the Ranch literature. It is described as a graveyard of sorts: ten old, big-body Cadillacs buried nose-down in a cemeterial row on a plot of unremarkable west Texas hardpan.

In addition to getting my picture, the plan is to walk around this graveyard in a sad little circle, deep and solemn feelings in my heart for all the personal dead I've lately neglected. All of them, but in particular my friend Todd Balloon, who floated back into the frame last night on the drive from Austin to Amarillo, some of the roads on that route so cracked and weather-beaten I thought they might at any point conclude in sand. For a while Todd was ghosting off at the edge of my headlight reach, out there with the mesquite brush and other bonelike High Plains growth. Todd, preserved in time in his ironed jeans rigged with thumbtacks, because he did not care for a rolled cuff. We had nothing new to say to each other, of course, but I was glad to have him. Todd was good company. The roads at that hour were lonely, the traffic going by in pieces—a car, a stillness, a truck, another stillness. Not really traffic at all. I had my coffee and weed, my cigarettes and sunflower seeds and talk radio, and, for a few miles, Todd, until a semi wiped out his ghost with its approach, high beams carving up the empty black. After the semi passed, a halo of residual light converted the road and the brush stuff bordering the road to bright mist. Once this faded the view ahead was exactly as unfamiliar as what I'd seen pre-semi, like driving through the fog of someone else's memory.

I don't explain to my lunch or dinner servers why, for my one day ever in Amarillo, Texas, I choose to eat at Hooters. They must get that all the time, men with their reasons. Mine are vague and sentimental, rooted in convenience—not unlike the restaurant itself, a theater of vague

sentimentality, walls papered over in kitsch that points back to simpler times in America, times that never actually happened.

There are more than 460 of these establishments located across the United States, each a chance to trade the here and now for an elsewhere located in the imagined past—to trade this Hooters in Amarillo for the one in your hometown, or Switzerland, or, for my purposes, the one in Jacksonville, Florida, situated between the apartment complex where I once lived and the call center where I once worked. Also the call center where Todd Balloon worked. He and I visited the Jax Hooters probably fewer than five times, and none of those times was an experience. But driving up through Texas last night, his haunt out there like some kind of Halloween vapor, it made me think maybe we'd had a moment there, here. And now I wonder how much chain restaurant revenue is attributable to revisionist nostalgia like this, how many people pick Mellow Mushroom or Bonefish Grill, On The Border or Olive Garden, Ruth's Chris or Morton's—how many pick these not for the food, which is sometimes extremely all right, but for the cushion of familiarity. How many prefer the known boundaries of a re-experience to the foreignness of the unexplored.

At the call center in Jacksonville, Todd and I did reduced-net-worth financial advisory. This was how the Firm titled it. The phrase meant something different then, during the ramp-up to the Housing Crash when the stock market was surging. We started the day after New Year's, 2006; fortunes were larger, roads to wealth wider and more direct.

Clients of the call center weren't rich and, in the Firm's estimation, were not on a trajectory to pile it up anytime soon. Traditional financial advisors out in the field had recruited these clients with the hope that they would make good, but it hadn't happened yet. So, the advisors who'd pursued them broke things off, sending their reduced-net-worthers to us at the FAC. Where before the client could go downtown and sit across from their advisor, name and title frosted across the glass, now they called an 800 number, keyed in the last four of their social, and were connected with total strangers. The images of us on their monthly statements depicted white, black, Asian, Latino men and women wearing headsets, dressed business formal, smiling the smile of the compassionate financial professional.

Such as Todd, with his fleshy cheeks and fine white teeth. He performed best on the phone, he believed, if he got his mind right during his morning commute. Not every day, but a lot of days. He had blondish hair, blue eyes, skin that went from pale to burned to pale again, no tan interlude, and yet he claimed a rich Italian heritage. Balloon, he said, was a dumbshit Americanization of Pallone. His ancestors, it was known, had been instrumental in the renovation of Naples. Todd's father, through whom the legacy ran, had a mother who cooked pasta right, her gravy touched with the urge of the homeland.

Following the FAC training period, Todd invited me down to Sunday lunch at the Balloons'. His parents lived in Gainesville, their neighborhood the kind where the houses are allowed small amounts of individuality, but the yards aren't. Todd's mother cooked spaghetti *arrabbiata,* the excess of which we sopped with olive bread. Red wine to drink. Afterward there was *sambuca* or *limoncello,* your preference. After that, standing on Todd's childhood driveway in the typically miserable central Florida late-spring heat with the hot food and drink in your stomach, the sun beating you on top

of the head, sweat making you too aware of your socked feet. Mr. Balloon was unaffected by these conditions. He could've eaten the meal outside, no shade. On the driveway he gave his report of the world, Todd nodding along, waiting his turn. Already the son showed signs of following the father's lead physically—Todd had a starter paunch, receding hairline, a sprinkle of sunspots on his forearms—and if he'd lived, he might've adopted Mr. Balloon's opinions, too. At least some. Todd felt strongly about his father and the hold he had on issues of importance. The thing wasn't to be right, Todd felt, but convincing.

Almost daily the FAC managerial bureau sent out a sheet of metrics that explained to the decimal point what you, Advisor #4606, had done with your yesterday. On these sheets you could click a button and see last week, last month, month to date, year to date, target to date. It was a diary of productivity, the entries written by the Firm in the artless language of numbers. Everybody abided this format. We learned how to translate those metrics sheets into a single, personal number that could be imagined floating over our heads, the same as you see in televised horse-racing games.

This fiscal calendar, important as it was, remained secondary to the holiday calendar, which granted us by law paid time off whenever the market shut. We all knew all the days we got. This woman who worked in the cube adjacent to mine decided in early December that working for the FAC was a soulsuck and that she couldn't do another hour of it, but, determined not to leave holiday money on the table— Christmas, New Year's, MLK—she

stayed through mid-February, turning in her notice the Tuesday after Presidents' Day. Such practice was not uncommon. People would work a month with quit in their hearts in order to get one unworked Monday paid in full. In this way the year passed, and, some twelve bonus cycles after that Sunday lunch at the Balloons', Todd and I began our second and final summer of service at the FAC.

The summer I'm talking about, 2007, the market climbing higher but now with a shadow of concern visible beneath its steep angle, was months of wet heat and lightning storms that dropped across Jacksonville with the sound and precision of bombs. These storms formed at time-lapse speeds, struck, and then took off as fast as they'd visited. Sometime that season Todd got placed on the warning shift, the one p.m. to ten p.m. time slot, the shift meant to reawaken in the employee the vigor of his new-hire days. It was the closest thing the FAC had to demotion, working those bad hours. Nobody wanted it except maybe the advisor who didn't want the job to begin with. Not starting until one in the afternoon, you missed the occasional catered lunch: buffet trays of barbecue, chicken parm, tacos, pasta salad so congealed that you could cut a chunk of it. And when staying late, long after market close, few revenue calls came in. Instead you spoke with the lonelies, those without jobs or lovers or passions distracting enough to keep the jobless loverlessness at bay and who needed to call late, to hear a voice before bed; and with the shitbirds, who didn't like the day to end without a fight; and to those living on the West Coast.

Todd struggled with it. He was struggling before being sent down, and then once on the warning shift, his metrics sank. A recession of one.

Plenty of days you could pull up his trade sheet and find it blank. Maybe he was out of the office, you thought, knowing better.

"What do they want me to do?" Todd said. "When I'm on inbounds it's all whiners and depressives. Outbounds, everyone's like, 'Listen, call me back in the fall.' The fall! Motherfucker, I won't have a job in the fall because of clients like you."

By one p.m., regardless of activity, Todd was damp with sweat—the oveny heat, his stocky bulk—and felt, he said, like he'd already worked a full day. His lunch break was a retiree's dinner. Late, when it got real slow, I suggested that instead of refreshing the handful of decent websites the Firm hadn't firewalled, maybe he might want to read.

"You know what I read?" Todd said. I didn't.

"The crawl on the bottom of the screen. News, sports. Keeps me sharp."

Anyway, Todd didn't have time for pleasure novels. All it took to turn a month from bottom percentile to top five, metrics-wise, was a couple good calls, and he wanted to be ready for them. Alert and undistracted. Also there was a woman in his life now, Laura. She commanded a large amount of his thinking, including the part where literature might've gone. Laura worked with us at the FAC in Compliance, and when she and Todd first picked up, she was engaged to another advisor. Very quickly that engagement dissolved. Todd felt bad about it but recognized that the situation was unavoidable, given his Italian blood.

get out to the Cadillac Ranch, though, and walking around the cars in a pose of dour reflection, as planned, realize I'm not so sure about the chronology. As in, maybe Laura happened sooner. Maybe she and Todd became a fixture that winter, or during his Good Friday Goodness party, and just sort of

stayed on through summer. I don't really know. I wasn't tracking Todd's life as closely as I'm making it sound, because, like everyone, I had my own little cupboard of worries to tend. Such as a bad month on the phones, after which would follow the warning shift and then getting clipped from a job I was embarrassed to have. How the ducks on the retention pond outside my apartment—property management called it a "lake"—had disappeared. All those works of genius I wouldn't write because I had a mind that stuck on call center metrics and ducks instead of epic human struggle.

What I do remember clearly is Todd getting this chest rash that quickly started to flame up his neck. He said it was heat-related, but I've come to think it was anxiety. If so, his last living months were spent in a weather of stress severe enough to boil the skin. Here at the Ranch, just yards from old Route 66, I would like to lay some blame at the feet of the call center's management, who kept after Todd, criticizing his prickly Latin manner on the phone, and who were so fixated on meeting quotas—revenue, production, calls handled per hour, per shift, per month, per quarter—that many knew us not by name but by our four-digit advisor handles. That's what I'd like, but those managers, citing their own anxieties, could point to the managers above them, who could point to the Board, who could point to the shareholders, who could point to America. And then it doesn't make sense, saying that America shot down my friend. Or that America was exploiting him, which is what's going on here, I suppose. Were Todd still alive, I doubt he'd feature much in this recount. I'd have had to call up a different ghost out there in the long, dark blank of west Texas or, failing that, be more honest about who I'm now trying to resurrect.

The rash kept Todd out of the office a few days and depleted his personals,

the sick days having been exhausted months ago. He came back, his neck still a little splotchy, and said this, which I must be editing to my taste, even though I can see it coming out of Todd's plump and sweat-smeared face: "Sometimes I just want to e-mail these clients our investment menu and tell them to print it out and throw a dart. Call me back with whatever you hit and I'll buy it in your account. What's it matter? All this stuff's the same. This guy the other day, he asked me the difference between two funds I was pushing. I thought I'd give him a choice—you know, let him feel good about making a decision. He said, 'What's the difference?' And I said, 'Well, one fund uses a lot of yellow in their advertising, and the other relies on a slogan. Both air commercials during golf tournaments.' And he said, 'Yeah, but what do they invest in?' I said, 'They invest in stuff that makes money, which right now is just about everything. They invest in steel and telecom and Brazil and Apple and defense contractors. They invest in companies you can't pronounce and in countries where people like you and me get shot on sight. More than anything else, though, they invest in companies that do investments. That's where the growth is.' The guy said, 'I need to think it over. I'll call you back in a few weeks.' I said, 'Fine. You've got eighteen grand to your name. Do you really think you're going to figure out money in a few weeks?' Nine o'clock at night and this guy has dick going on. People like that can't make decisions, even when it's not even a decision at all."

n conflict with FAC best practice, Todd was released on a Wednesday. Even Laura, who you'd think would've been made aware of an imminent firing up there in the Compliance empyrean, seemed surprised by the timing. If she knew, she didn't let on, and the day it

happened she signed out of her workstation at six p.m. on the number and drove fast to Todd's apartment, ready to comfort.

This was around what should've been the conclusion of that heat-sogged summer, approaching Labor Day, which Todd was compensated for in his slender severance package, the minimum allowed by the regulatory powers that be. Most of the country had moved into fall, concerning themselves with long sleeves and the start of the finish of another year, but for Todd the holiday and the season it launched were passed in the pursuit of work, rather than the temporary suspension of it.

Unemployment at that time, the third quarter of 2007, was so slight as to be an economic abstraction. When asked, Todd said that he was between jobs, an answer that, in the heart of the boom, sounded like a new kind of profanity. He took the bright side, though, at least outwardly. An FAC-less future was possible again, he said. He could go back to school, learn Italian, be a better uncle, or maybe join the military full bore—he'd attended the Naval Academy for two years—as long as they could look past his bum knee. And he still had Laura, who took Todd out drinking whenever he got low.

Todd decided that he and Laura would marry. It was time; he now liked the idea of a wife. Before talking to Laura about it, Todd went ahead and established his groomsmen, planting the idea in our minds early. This was his present to us, that of being on the inside of a secret.

It was also important that Todd get his news in circulation before leaving Jacksonville. After a few months on the search, he'd found work in his hometown of Gainesville, just far enough away that commuting was impractical. A girlfriend might not move with him, but a fiancée would. He'd go down in advance of Laura to set things up, and once steady income was proven, she'd follow. There was plenty for her to like in Gainesville, Todd said. It wasn't coastal Florida, but maybe that was better. Maybe if the beach weren't always an option, to the point that going becomes an obligation, a chore akin to exercising, then maybe you savor it more the few times you schedule it out, make the drive, and plant your umbrella in the far sand, away from the crush of the tourists and the young. Plus it was cheaper inland. No beach-city housing prices like what you found in Jax.

Todd's final point was that his parents liked Laura. They approved of the match. This was important. His parents had been married a hundred years and therefore understood the institution backward and front. Todd would be married the rest of his life, he knew, commitment being hereditary in the Balloon family, so it was important that he get this part—the wife part—right.

Whether Todd and Laura ever officially got engaged was unclear, at least to me. He moved down to Gainesville; I left the FAC and the South for New York City. Not long after, the stock market—still my field—began to shudder. No one made much of it at first, because it didn't make sense that an economy plowing on stuff as tangible as housing could crater without giving clear, fair warning. It was illogical. And no fun to think about. Down in Florida, no longer home, whole neighborhoods continued to bloom overnight. You could see them from the highways—those gardens of themed tract homes, red and blue and green and off-white residential flowers. In the cities were condo-tower skeletons like gray trellises. Construction cranes made new skylines. Later, after Todd passed, it was towers partially completed, high stacks of raw concrete awaiting a finish that wasn't coming.

"Imagine," Todd said, "walking into a bank fifty years ago and saying, 'I don't have savings, my salary sometimes doesn't even cover my monthly expenses, but I was wondering if you could maybe loan me a house.'" This was a phone call over Thanksgiving, HoneyBaked Ham and thawed sides on the table, gifts my mother had sent to yet another new address of mine, this one on West Fifty-Seventh Street. Todd was doing something with mortgages in Gainesville, work I didn't really understand. There was little I could tell him about New York that he didn't already know; he'd lived in Boca Raton and, because of this, had a fixed idea of what he called "city life." The hard November weather up north, familiar to Todd from his Academy days in Annapolis, was another settled topic. His people, from southern Italy, not good sufferers of winter, had passed down to him their disdain for the cold.

We traded notes like this for a bit, and then one day in March I got a real bad call. The kind of call that, in our headset days, Todd and I would've transferred to the Legal Team, who were required to deal with Unexpected Tragedies. It was on the FAC Responsibilities Chart. Legal handled all the paperwork—wills, beneficiaries, powers of attorney—and they'd had to pass an empathy test, too. Professional helpers of the bereaved, which I was not. Nor Todd. I'd like to think that if the situation were reversed, if someone had called him to say that I'd been found dead, alone in my apartment, the TV on and nothing but my usual diet of after-work intoxicants present on the coffee table, he wouldn't have known what to do either.

Todd's funeral, postponed for two months, took place the summer after the Jacksonville summer I've been telling about. Why such a delay I'm not sure, but it suggested that the family was as confused about next steps as the friends were. When we did gather—the weekend after Memorial Day, a date the family determined worked best for the most—I don't think there was a coffin, which by that point would have been pretense. It was strange, summoning up whatever you'd felt months ago and presenting it there to the public in the hot still of a central Florida church. The emotions were dated. In that way we the attendees were re-enacting, pretending that in the interim between the Unexpected Tragedy and now, we'd held this feeling, our funeral feeling, *this* close, and that in that time managed to stay our obsessions, suspending the wanting of the things we wanted, pleasure and quiet and success, happiness and revenge and approval and understanding and everything else. Like we'd been wearing sad this whole time, real as these dark suits.

The priest in charge acknowledged early in the ceremony that several months had passed between expiry and burial, letting everyone off the hook. You could hear the pews creak when he said it, people untightening themselves. Laura sat near the front; she was poised but visibly shaken. I wondered what her current status was with the family, and what it would become. After the service the church provided snacks and refreshments, including spaghetti with marinara sauce. "Strips of particle board topped with chunky ketchup," said a Balloon.

Before leaving the Ranch I take a long stare from a distance, standing way back, far enough away that the Cadillacs look less like classic automobiles half-sunk in hardpan than they do the ribs of some dead, nightmare beast, the rest of his carcass having been picked clean. There is a wind blowing firm and steady across the flat, stirring up the dirt and knocking over empty spray-paint cans but making no progress against the art itself. There are ten Cadillacs, each a slightly different vintage, though all of them look to have been built during the moon-shot generation. They're buried in such a way, we're told, as to slant the same slant as the Great Pyramid of Giza, perhaps a comment on empire.

All of the cars have been comprehensively tagged: declarations of love across a trunk; varsity pride on the door; dates and initials; praise for Jesus; a thick red dollar sign punctuating a quote against capitalism. So much graffiti that it is now the fabric of the cars; there's too much for any of it to mean anything on its own. I think of Todd's last car, a Lincoln. He bought it used after being fired from the FAC, thinking a fat, stately sedan would send the signal that he was serious about his future, a future that on the surface looked a little like the past. He was moving back to Gainesville but wasn't coming home tail tucked, the Lincoln said.

Had he survived the rest of that calendar year, Todd could've driven it through the heart of the crash, past all those residential towers and subdivision builders stamped into the Florida swampland one after the next. It was a tough catastrophe to connect with, the economic fallout of 2008. There was no physical destruction, no fire or flood, and while it was clear that many very unfortunate, often defenseless citizens were under attack, the extent of the damage done was harder to see. And the villains weren't really new, either. Bankers, traders, venal regulators—those we always suspect of some kind of fuckery. We did learn of a new kind of minority in the U.S., the subprime borrower. Statistically it was likely you either knew one of them or were one, those unrich Americans who coveted their own homes. Things would get bad for them. They'd have it worse than the bank who had loaned them money or the brokerage firm who had bundled their mortgage with a mess of other mortgages and then sold tranches of that bundle to a different brokerage firm, who sold back to the original firm some tranches of its own. A couple years later, though, the news would move on, and the crash, once finished crashing, could be seen as a hurdle stumbled over during the great golden race to providence.

Todd would've enjoyed those days, grim as some of them were. He'd done work on both ends of the meltdown, mortgage brokerage and financial advisory, and I imagine he'd have liked to take credit for his involvement. How many FAC clients had he talked into buying mutual funds heavy on real estate and financial services, even on the warning shift. Enough to buy a used Lincoln, I guess. I never saw that car, but I imagine that in terms of style it beats my faux SUV, which I now reboard. The tourist picture is taken, and I'm ready to be on the road again. The sun is setting, reminding me how long lunch at the Amarillo Hooters was, and I have a go-cup of coffee in my cup holder, compliments of the dinner server. She was concerned about the remainder of my trip, both the length left to California and the condition of the driver tasked with covering it by himself. But I was all right, I told her. I do my best driving late, after dark, when the lonelies and the shitbirds and the spirits of recent past come out to celebrate the night. LP

FAST FOOD
BY SCOTT KORB   **PHOTOGRAPHS BY LIZ BARCLAY**

One late afternoon last June, a few weeks before the start of Ramadan, with an hour remaining before *Asr*, Islam's afternoon prayer, Imam Khalid Latif became suddenly aware of blood on his shirt. Even though he was on the road, he knew he would have to pray soon but was not sure that he could.

Five daily prayers constitute a pillar of Islam, and these prayers are to be done in a state of ritual purity. To this end, Muslims wash before they pray, a preparation known as *wudhu* that includes careful attention to the

hands, mouth, nose, face, arms, hair, ears, and feet. The clothes you wear are supposed to be clean, too. The stain on his shirt was a problem.

The imam had begun the day with a prayer at sunrise. Soon after, accompanied by a friend, he'd left New York City in a van headed for a halal meat–processing facility in western Maryland known as Simply Natural, about 250 miles away. By one o'clock that afternoon, the men had packed the vehicle with three hand-slaughtered steers and were headed back.

"Let's not stop," the imam had said somewhere along the way.

Latif had no change of clothes. Anticipating the logjam on the New Jersey side of the Holland Tunnel, he started calling sheikhs for advice.

After two or three calls, he reached Dawood Yasin, an imam from Berkeley, California, and an avid bow hunter familiar with the mess involved in breaking down animals. After some consideration, Yasin had an answer. Drawing on a tradition of Islamic legal scholarship, he said, "For the butcher, the blood, it's considered pure." He then thought more. "Let me ask my wife, just in case."

The story ends in a sort of anticlimax. Traffic was light enough that Latif and his friend arrived at their destination in time for a change of clothes. They had time not only to prepare themselves for prayer, but to unload the van, too.

Still, after some debate between Sheikh Dawood and his wife, they'd come to an agreement: the prayer would have been permissible, although the sheikh seems to have overstated the case at first. The legal principle in question doesn't purify impure blood; it excuses the Muslim caught in a situation he simply can't avoid. By profession, the butcher gets covered in blood. And the imam was now a butcher. Or, close enough—since March he'd owned a meat shop.

In the summer of 2010, I began chronicling the inaugural year of Zaytuna College, the nation's first four-year Muslim liberal arts school; this is when I first met Sheikh Dawood Yasin. When, in April 2013, two brothers set off bombs near the finish line of the Boston Marathon, I collaborated with Suhaib Webb, imam of New England's largest mosque, on an op-ed for the *New York Times*, where we argued that the country's mainstream Islamic institutions are essential to fighting religious extremism. Though not Muslim myself, I've come to see Islam as an increasingly significant—and often misunderstood—influence on American civic life.

In this spirit and with this story in mind, I spent a lot of time at Latif's butcher shop this past Ramadan, Islam's holy month, when Muslims refrain from all food and drink from sunrise to sunset. Like Dawood Yasin, the scholars at Zaytuna College, and Suhaib Webb, Khalid Latif has, over the years, been a helpful guide into the tradition, specifically my understanding of Ramadan. So has the convert Rollo Romig, a Muslim writer who has become a friend. Writing for the *New Yorker* about his first Ramadan fast in 2012, Romig explained that, unlike other religious fasting, this long month of long days is "intended primarily for focus and elevation, not for penance and atonement. It's not about mortification of the flesh or otherwise beating yourself up—Ramadan is really about developing new habits: of thought, action, routine. The extremity

of the test is what makes it so vivid."

Visiting Latif's shop throughout the month, a question took shape in my mind: What could make the fast more vivid for a Muslim—the month more purifying—than living it in a food store, offering recipes, wrapping up burgers, and hearing customers talk of midday summer barbecues while you go without?

At thirty-two, Khalid Latif is relatively young for an imam, and shorter than he seems, a New Jersey native whose family emigrated from Pakistan in the 1970s. He opened the store, Honest Chops, with three partners. They've since hired a few other employees. It's the first whole-animal halal butcher shop in the country.

After graduating in 2004 from New York University, where I teach and where the imam and I initially met, Latif studied at Hartford Seminary's

ABOVE: Imam Khalid Latif; his butcher shop, Honest Chops.

Islamic Chaplaincy Program—also the first of its kind in the nation. His main work as a religious leader has been with the New York Police Department—in 2007, he was named the city's Muslim chaplain—and as the imam overseeing NYU's Islamic Center, an appointment he's held since 2005.

His business partners at Honest Chops are members of his congregation, which is open to Muslims with or without an affiliation with NYU. Twenty-five percent of the store's profits will go back into the Islamic Center. Being a Muslim leader in this country now often involves the cultivation of Islamic institutions committed to social services, education, devotion, activism, or the arts. Honest Chops was founded, in part, to help fund

job-training programs, a domestic violence shelter, and an Islamic school in Manhattan. These projects are likewise financially supported by a Muslim wedding service and some Edible Arrangements franchises.

The thought to open a whole-animal butcher shop in the East Village came to Latif and his wife during Ramadan 2013. They had encountered problems getting halal food they considered wholesome. One variation of the story—a version of which Latif wrote as part of his annual Ramadan reflections for the *Huffington Post*—has his wife "bewildered" at halal meat counters, where butchers try to sell her cuts she hasn't ordered, or aren't familiar with the cuts she wants, or "cut the meat, pick up the phone, use the cash register, and blow their nose simultaneously, all without gloves on."

Latif told me about his own experience that same summer in a meat shop on Atlantic Avenue in Brooklyn, a stretch of which is packed with Islamic and Middle Eastern markets. Latif was there with Anas Hasan, now thirty, a partner in the shop who at the time was working as a baggage handler for United Airlines and seeking some direction in his life. The pair was basically being ignored. "The butcher is picking up huge slabs of meat," Latif told me, "and there's a pile of meat in the corner, about ten, fifteen feet away from him, and how it's getting there is, he's picking pieces up from the box and throwing them against the wall. And they're ricocheting against the wall into that pile. And it's just building up. Every few minutes he's scratching his beard, rubbing his nose." This meat is halal, but the imam can't bring himself to bring it home.

Now, on the one hand, what offended Latif could be seen as a basic lack of hygiene. Offensive to most anyone. But from an Islamic perspective, the problem with the Atlantic Avenue butchery—and "the stories could go on and on," Latif says—is that it lacks "real excellence," or *ihsan*, a word derived from a root in Arabic that denotes beauty, perfection, and spiritual fulfillment.

Ihsan is meant to be a constant pursuit for believers. To help out, Allah gives the believer a month each year, Ramadan, to focus; daily fasting is a physical reminder of one's spiritual commitments. Breaking fast with an evening meal, or *iftar*, relieves the hunger and the thirst, but only temporarily, because it also prepares the believer for the following day's hunger and thirst. And breaking fast within a community, which is often how it's done—at iftars prepared and served by volunteers, with food paid for through donations—tells the Muslim he is not alone in his daily pursuit.

And yet, Latif's encounter on Atlantic Avenue suggests something else entirely. There's no in-it-togetherness when the halal butcher shows neither you nor the animals he sells any of the sympathy Islam calls him to. And it's a real shame. Not doing one's best during Ramadan is to miss the opportunity Allah has provided for believers to focus on elevating—even perfecting—their lives. For Latif, opening a butcher shop is about taking what halal *can* mean—meat thrown across the room, swarming flies, a stench, careless cuts—and trying to elevate it. Make it better, more wholesome, more pure. Can what Allah has deemed permissible be made more perfect? As a time set apart from the rest of the year, Ramadan presents this possibility as a challenge and confronts the believer with the potential for a human to become more perfect—better than he is.

RIGHT: David Hurtado cuts meat; Anas Hasan is the face of Honest Chops.

For practicing Muslims, the Koran provides the basic principles governing the lawfulness of all things in the world and of all human activity. That's a lot. The book's second chapter, *Surat al-Baqarah* ("The Cow"), includes this line: "It is He who created for you all of that which is on the earth." "He" is God, or Allah. *Surat al-Jathiyah,* the book's forty-fifth chapter, contains this: "And He has subjected to you whatever is in the heavens and whatever is on the earth—all are from Him." These lines are often interpreted as revealing the mercy of Allah, whose gifts to humanity—"all of that which is on the earth"—are understood to be endless. When Muslims invoke the name of God with the refrain *Bismillah ar-Rahman ar-Raheem*, a phrase that opens all but one of the chapters of the Koran, they're saying, "In the name of Allah, the Beneficent, the Merciful."

For Muslims, just as the Koran presents God's generosity and mercy in establishing what humanity may do and what on earth we're allowed to use or eat, so too does the book set limits on what God considers lawful. All things are permissible, or halal, unless they've been identified by God as forbidden, or *haram*. He says no pork. No carrion. No booze. No blood that gushes forth from an animal. Adherence to these distinctions shapes the moral life. And in the moral universe of the slaughterhouse, where an overwhelming majority of halal animals in this country become haram when they're shot with a captive bolt pistol, a blessing and a sharp knife make all the difference to the Muslim. For Latif, a little more mercy would make a greater difference still.

A convert named Abdush Shakur slaughters goats and lambs and chickens and steers for Simply Natural in a low, white concrete building where he and I met in late July. I asked how his Ramadan was going. "*Alhamdulillah,*" he said. All praise is due to Allah. "I can't complain."

Proper slaughter makes the animals he kills halal. When they're calm, they're said to have submitted to Allah. The attention this slaughterhouse pays to animal welfare helps ensure that the meat is wholesome, or *tayyib*. The day I visited, I found three young steers Shakur had slaughtered, all split right down the middle and aging in the freezer. Two animals of about the same size—close to 650 pounds each—white fat over their flesh, had been raised and finished on grass; between them hung a huge grain-finished steer whose fat had turned golden. Latif had been assured that on the farms—both in Maryland and in western Pennsylvania's Amish country—all of Simply Natural's animals are given room to roam and grass to eat (even if they're finished on grain). Taken together with their eventual halal slaughter, these qualities are what bring Latif all the way to Sharpsburg, Maryland, for his beef. Honest Chops's goal is to bring the halal butcher shop up to the same standard as your modern-day artisanal meat counter.

Shakur, whose daily task is known as *dhabihah*, is forty-six and lives in Hagerstown, Maryland. He is stout, black, with close-cropped hair and a white-fringed beard. He has the word KHARI tattooed on his right hand, presumably from a time before he became a Muslim; according to the *hadith*—the tradition of words and acts of the Prophet—tattoos are haram. Shakur took the *shahadah* (declared himself a Muslim) during Ramadan 1995. He'd been reading literature sent by an incarcerated brother. Still, he told me, "When I accepted Islam, I didn't understand Islam. It took me years and years and years and years to get it. I was a Muslim, but I wasn't acting in accordance with Islam all the time until maybe ten years ago, when I devoted my life to Islam."

This was about the time he left his work as a carpenter and electrician and started killing animals

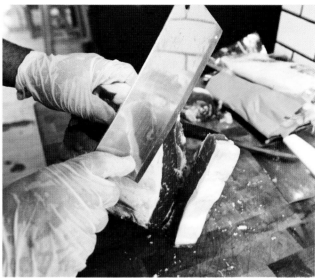

HONEST CHOPS
whole animal butcher
all-natural ⟶ locally sourced

in the name of God. Moving from Washington, D.C., in 2004, he found work through his brother-in-law in a halal slaughterhouse elsewhere in Washington County. He found in his colleagues a model of how to live. "I see the way these people move, the way they act, and as I read the Koran and the *sunnah*," Shakur explained, using the Arabic term for the normative way of life for the Muslim, as transmitted by the hadith, "I started seeing that it coincided with what they were doing." Those slaughterers revealed to him what it looked like to be a Muslim. "It was by the grace of Allah that Allah allowed me to go there," he told me. He also said it was an accident.

These days, now at Simply Natural, a smaller operation, when there are animals in the barn out back, he shares the slaughter floor with a USDA inspector named Alan. This is solitary and tiring work, particularly during the Ramadan fast. One at a time, animals move from the barn through an alley into a "squeeze chute," their shoulders forcing a gate around their necks as they step forward. When the steer is in this position, and it's calm, Shakur will recite the words "*Bismillah Allahu Akbar*"—in the name of Allah, God is great—and then he'll kill it with one pass of a sharp blade through the jugulars, the windpipe, and the esophagus. It's preferable if the knife remains hidden from view until the slaughter. "One thing about Muslims," he explained, "is that we try to remember Allah all the time. Doing this type of work—halal killing—it makes you remember Allah because you glorify all day. Even with the kills—you're glorifying Allah all day."

H onest Chops is set below street level on Ninth Street in New York's East Village. Since opening this past spring, Anas Hasan has become the de facto face of the store. It's given him direction and focus—this Ramadan he was

studying Ryan Farr's *Whole Beast Butchery*—yet he's maintained his part-time work at the airport for the perk of free travel.

Behind the counter, Hasan is cheery, a glad-hander without the smarm. People recognize him on the street, and he recognizes them. There is a mosque a few blocks away, but most of his customers, he says, are not Muslim. A shingle hangs out front of the store reading HALAL BUTCHER, but Hasan explains that for most passersby a different sign above the lintel and a sandwich board on the sidewalk make the more impressive argument for shopping here: ALL-NATURAL CHICKEN, GRASS-FED BEEF, LOCALLY SOURCED. The shop is making no obvious effort to convert non-Muslims to Islam. But the door is open in other ways and for other reasons just as central to the faith.

Customers on Atlantic Avenue buy meat from the halal shop Latif described because they have to; those shoppers are Muslims in search of food that is permissible to eat. The shop owner can get away with throwing meat across a room only if he doesn't really want outsiders to come in. For Honest Chops, the impulse is clearly different. The inspiration may still come from Brooklyn, but it's the Brooklyn of whole-animal butchery and farm-to-table cuisine. In this way, it's American Islam without other apparent kinds of ethnic attachments. Of course, a broad appeal in an increasingly prosperous neighborhood is better for business, and building a strong business benefits the partners while also feeding the Islamic community and institution they all belong to. But it also reflects a much more expansive sense of Islamic mercy than we find in the shared sympathy of the Ramadan fast, the fellowship of an iftar, or even the establishment of a school for Muslim children. Inviting others in and serving them what they want—in this case, well-raised organic meats,

cut to order—fulfills what Dr. Umar Faruq Abd-Allah, a well-regarded scholar from Chicago, has called the "cultural imperative" within Islam. Looking back through history and across the world, Dr. Umar says that, "In China, Islam looked Chinese; in Mali, it looked African." In the East Village in 2014, Islam should look like the East Village. And as dealers in meat, the proprietors of Honest Chops must reflect a culture whose growing disgust at industrial farming has reshaped the moral universe of the farm, the slaughterhouse, the butcher shop, and the kitchen.

Over the centuries, Dr. Umar argues in a widely read 2004 essay, the advantages for Muslims of following this cultural imperative have been profound. "The religion," he writes, "became not only functional and familiar at the local level but dynamically engaging, fostering stable indigenous Muslim identities and allowing Muslims to put down deep roots and make lasting contributions wherever they went." Honest Chops is already talking about franchises and the possibility of running their own abattoir; they seem to believe in both broad engagement and carving out a place for oneself. To take root, their Islam recommends both things in equal measure.

R amadan ends with Eid al-Fitr, the Feast of Breaking the Fast, which Latif and his congregation celebrated on Monday, July 28. In the spirit of engaging with the community at large, and because their own space for worship had grown too small to suit their needs, they arranged for morning prayers and a brunch to take place in Judson Memorial Church, a Christian congregation with its own long history of public engagement, including opening its doors to Occupy Wall Street protestors evicted from Zuccotti Park following a police raid in November 2011.

When I arrived outside Judson the

morning of Eid, the line of those waiting to be admitted extended along Washington Square South and around the corner, far down Thompson Street. A little after nine, when the doors opened and the crowds began streaming in, each worshipper was handed a plastic deli bag for his shoes. Attendees had been asked to bring their own prayer rugs, and as they entered they formed rows of men toward the front, women in the back. The 2,000-square-foot sanctuary, plus the balcony, began filling up quickly. In most mosques I've been to there's at least a narrow walkway separating the men and women. This was not the case at Judson.

For Eid, Honest Chops had supplied the caterer with meat for chicken tikka, which would be arranged in warming pans alongside rice, chickpeas and beans, flatbread, fruit, and the sweet semolina dessert, halva. Sweets, in particular, are a traditional part of the Eid celebration—a unique day for Muslims when fasting is not allowed. Someone had donated boxes of Dunkin' Donuts. There was a massive container of organic dates.

Filling the church took most of an hour. Latif, who would lead the celebration, worried aloud about the crush of families. Dressed in a flowing golden robe and head covering, he positioned himself at the head of the congregation at a spot near the back of the sanctuary, so that the worshippers would be facing Mecca.

"Sisters," he said, "I don't mean this in an offensive way, but can you move backwards?" There was some movement. "Pray really, really close to each other," he encouraged. "If you need to make *sajdah*"—prostrations—"on someone's back, it's permissible," he said.

All the while, the sound of the *Eid Takbirs*, a sung pronouncement of God's greatness—"*Allahu Akbar, Allahu Akbar, Allahu Akbar*"—murmured through the hall.

Eventually everyone would make it in, piling into the sanctuary, the balcony, three staircases, a foyer, and a lower-level hall. The crowd, including many small children, reached nearly two thousand people. Latif's prayers and his sermon were broadcast over a cell phone into the basement; a member of the congregation would relay the start of each new prayer cycle into the stairwells in a game of long-distance Telephone.

For a month, these men and women had lived in the shared sympathy and the vivid fellowship of the fast. The month had been an opportunity for them to practice doing their best. But Ramadan was now over. And before he let them go—back into their pre-Ramadan lives and routines, their old thoughts and actions—Latif wanted to remind them of what they'd all just been through, and why.

"Carry forth with you what you have taken from Ramadan as a starting point," he said. "And let consciousness and mindfulness be the criteria by which you move forward." Doing so, he said, means making one's particular life more perfect, continuing in the spirit of Ramadan even after it's gone, and then showing up for those around—Muslim or not—so that their lives may be improved. "We will not benefit from the blessing that is uniquely you if you are not here for us to be able to take benefit from it."

The community, he said, was moving in different directions. Continuing to build. "But there is still a lot of work to be done," he added. "And we want to build something that reaches its pinnacle and its best, and when that's done we want to keep building and keep growing." Here was the relentless striving toward ihsan. There is a free clinic in the works, and the shelter for women who face violence at home. Honest Chops was part of the growth and had also paid into the kitty.

Latif's prayers went on. He called to Allah. The congregation's *ameens* tumbled after in call-and-response. And Latif remembered: "There are people in this world, they will not have food to eat in celebration of this day of Eid." All of us would. "*Ya Allah*," he said, "grant them and their loved ones and all of us the best of meals in the world beyond this one."

Ameen.

The imam looked over the congregation. "Make this a blessed day for all of you; feel free to hug each other. We have brunch after." **LP**

The highly anticipated debut cookbook
from Christopher Kostow, chef at
The Restaurant at Meadowood

AVAILABLE EVERYWHERE BOOKS ARE SOLD

@tenspeedpress | TEN SPEED PRESS | tenspeedpress.com

CHRISTMAS IN INDIA

RECIPES BY
MICHAEL SNYDER

PHOTOGRAPHS BY
MAREN CARUSO

In the opening scene of the apocryphal Acts of Thomas, written in the early third century, the apostles are sitting around after the death and resurrection of their Lord and Savior, drawing lots to decide who will spread the good word where. Judas Thomas draws India and balks, "saying that by reason of the weakness of the flesh he could not travel." Even when Christ personally commands him, Thomas waffles: "Where you would send me, send me," he says, "but elsewhere, for to the Indians I will not go."

To the Indians he *does* go, of course, though only after Christ compels him to follow a merchant called Abbanes. After some high jinks on the journey east—including a memorable visit to an inn where a nasty cup-bearer is devoured by a lion and a comely Hebraic flautist throws herself at his feet—Thomas arrives on India's southwestern coast, at the port of Muziris in modern-day Kerala. He proceeds to travel around South India, performing miracles and conversions, founding seven churches and eventually dying a martyr with four spears in his abdomen. (Turns out those initial misgivings weren't unfounded.) The Basilica of San Thome in the city of Chennai is believed to stand on the site of the apostle's tomb.

A couple millennia later, Christians represent the second largest religious minority in India after Muslims in the predominantly Hindu nation. According to the 2001 census, there are more than 24 million Christians (about 2.3 percent of the population) in India, and they reside in the farthest corners of the country. The Syrian Christians in the southwest, where Thomas proselytized, have practiced the faith for longer than most Northern Europeans. Farther north, Christians along India's Arabian Sea coast from Mangalore to

Surat practice Roman Catholicism, first introduced by the Dominican missionary Jordanus in the fourteenth century and popularized (at least in part through financial incentives) by the Portuguese a century later. India's three majority-Christian states—the tribal hill states of Meghalaya, Mizoram, and Nagaland, evangelized by Protestant missionaries in the nineteenth century—all lie in the remote northeast, bordering Bangladesh and Burma. Smaller Christian communities also turn up among other tribal communities of the northeast, in the northwestern state of Punjab, and increasingly among the tribal *adivasis* (India's indigenous people) concentrated in the poorest regions of the central and eastern states.

The geographic and cultural diversity of these communities is reflected in their food. Goan-Catholic cuisine is heavily inflected with the flavors of Portugal. The East Indians of Bombay incorporate dishes of both Portuguese and British provenance. Christians in Kerala are famous for their beef preparations and rich coconut curries. Christians along the coast of the Arabian Sea specialize in pork. In the north-

east, and particularly in Nagaland, tribal communities are omnivorous, consuming, as one Naga friend put it to me (and only half-facetiously), "anything that moves."

During the holidays, in the south and west, communities with older Christian traditions feast on dishes that have become as central to Christmas as ham is stateside: a delicately spiced roast duck among Syrian Christians, for instance, and the variety of pork dishes made farther up the coast. For communities that converted more recently, Christmas cooking usually revolves around pre-Christian dishes typical to the region. In the northeast, where most conversion took place in the latter half of the nineteenth century, the pig slaughters that have been part of traditional celebrations practically forever became a central feature of the holiday, resulting in a preponderance of dishes that focus on minimally seasoned pork and offal.

Sourced from professional cooks and their relatives, from scribes of authoritative cookbooks and neighborhood aunties, the holiday recipes that follow—all of them more or less specific to Christmas—capture the tiniest of cross-sections of Indian Christendom, but still shine some light on the depth and diversity of that nebulous thing we call "Indian cuisine."

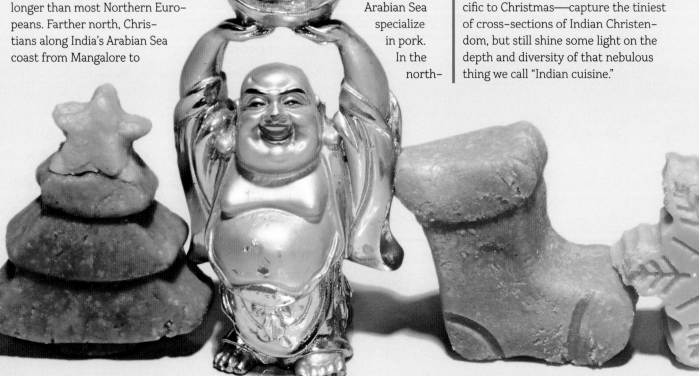

MARZIPAN

Adapted from Astrid Rodrigues | Makes about 2 lbs

In the eighteenth century, when the British East India Company replaced Portugal as the dominant power on Salsette Island north of Bombay, residents of the North Konkan district—the area in and around the city—called themselves East Indians as a sign of their new allegiance, despite living on India's western coast. East Indian cooking tends to reflect centuries of exposure to European cultures. In the weeks before Christmas, East Indian aunties from across the suburb of Bandra (once a set of fishing villages, now Bombay's most fashionable neighborhood) prepare British fruitcakes and homemade marzipan, adapted from the Portuguese. The Portuguese also introduced East Indians to cashews, and Christians in Bombay and Goa started using the locally grown nuts instead of expensive foreign almonds.

Like many East Indian women in Bandra, Astrid has been making marzipan and other Christmas sweets for years, making one batch to eat at home and others to sell by special order. She says a traditional East Indian Christmas feast would involve potato chops (breaded and fried mashed-potato patties stuffed with minced beef), a variety of sweets, and a roasted suckling pig. Genesia Alves, a friend of the Rodrigues family, told me that when she was a kid, some of the Muslim families that owned the neighborhood bakeries would actually rent out their big, professional ovens to roast the whole pigs, since urban households rarely had the appropriate implements. The deepening of ethno-religious tensions across the city in the last twenty years has pretty much eliminated that practice. These days, roasted chicken is a fairly common replacement for suckling pig on an East Indian Christmas table.

Before you begin: you will need a candy thermometer, a large bowl of cold water, and a cutting board, marble slab, or Silpat mat dusted in confectioners' sugar.

1 Combine the sugar and water in a heavy-bottomed pot large enough to hold all of the ingredients. Melt the sugar over a low flame while stirring gently.

2 Add the cream of tartar, raise the heat, cover the pot with a tight-fitting lid, and leave for 3 minutes.

3 Remove the lid and attach a candy thermometer. With the heat fairly high and without stirring, bring the syrup to 240°F, the soft-ball stage. Remove from heat and place the bottom of the pan in the waiting bowl of cold water. Stir the syrup quickly but carefully until it becomes cloudy white.

4 Working quickly, return the pot to the stove and mix in the nuts and egg whites. Reheat the mixture over a low flame while stirring to combine, about 2–3 minutes.

5 Turn the marzipan out onto the sugar-dusted surface. Using a wooden paddle or spatula, turn and fold it until it is cool enough to handle. Once it is, knead the dough for 5 or 6 minutes until smooth. You may need to add more confectioner's sugar; do so a tablespoon at a time. Let rest for an hour or two at room temperature.

6 Knead the mixture again. At this point, you can divide and dye the marzipan with food coloring and press it into silicone cookie molds. To make multicolored marzipan, as Astrid does, break the dough into blocks and color each with a few drops of food coloring. You can then place different colors of marzipan in the different sections of the molds (so you can make stamens and petals different colors in flowers, for instance). Astrid had a silicone mold made from Legos so she could make Lego-shaped marzipan for her grandchildren. She also makes fruit-shaped marzipan, which she molds by hand.

Serve immediately or wrap in plastic wrap and store in the fridge. The finished candies will keep for about 2 weeks.

2 C granulated sugar
⅔ C water
⅛ t cream of tartar
3 C cashew or almond meal, or a mixture
2 egg whites, lightly whisked
½ C confectioners' sugar, plus more for kneading
+ food coloring (optional)

MANGALOREAN PORK CURRY

Adapted from Julie D'Souza | Makes 6–8 Servings

Like Goa and Bombay to the north, Mangalore was heavily influenced by the Portuguese. Vasco da Gama landed not far from there in 1498, and from 1526 to 1640, the city came under Portuguese rule. The cooking here shows Portuguese influence, but not quite as strongly as in Goa, which remained part of Portugal until 1961. Much like other Luso-Indian dishes, this curry features vinegar and pork and is best served either with *pão*, a soft, Portuguese-style dinner roll, or steamed rice.

Julie D'Souza, who taught me this recipe, was also among the first people I met when I moved to Bombay nearly three years ago. At the time, I was living with an American couple in their apartment in the central Bombay neighborhood of Parel.

Julie was their housekeeper, and when I moved to the suburbs, she continued working with me, helping to keep my house tidy and showing me how to use the mysterious vegetables that I brought home from the market. This Mangalorean pork recipe has been passed down for generations and came to Julie through her mother-in-law. A typical Mangalorean Christmas feast features dishes from both southern and western India: *idli* or *dosa* (typical South Indian snacks made from fermented rice and lentil batters); *tendli* (a gourd that looks like a miniature cucumber) or chickpeas cooked with coconut, both common in West India; rice cooked with dried fruit and nuts; and a simple salad of chopped cucumber, tomato, and onion.

1 Marinate the pork: place the pork in a large pot (you're going to add a significant amount of liquid masala later and cook in the same pot, so make sure there's plenty of room). Grind the cloves, peppercorns, cinnamon, and star anise in a spice grinder or with a mortar and pestle. Use your hands to mix together the spices and remaining ingredients with the pork, then set aside while you prepare the masala.

2 Make the masala: dry-roast your ginger, garlic, and onion in a pan over a low flame. Once they start to wilt and sweat a little bit, add the whole spices, then the chilies. When the whole mixture has become aromatic, remove from heat.

3 Let the spice mixture cool, then scrape it into a blender along with turmeric and tamarind. Add ½ cup of water as you start to blend. Continue adding water and blending until the mixture forms a smooth liquid, roughly the color and texture of tomato soup (if you didn't manage to find the Kashmiri chilies, your liquid might not be quite tomato-red; add a few teaspoons of paprika). The idea here is to combine the spices as completely as possible so that there are no dangerously large pieces of any spice.

4 Once the masala paste is finished, add it to the pork and mix with your hands. Add water (about another ¾ cup) to the empty blender and pulse once or twice. Add this water to the pork. (It's okay if there's not enough liquid to completely submerge the pork.)

5 Add 2 tablespoons of vinegar and salt to taste, then cover and place over a high flame until the entire mixture comes to a boil. Once it boils, lower heat immediately and continue to simmer for about 45 minutes, stirring occasionally. The curry is ready when the meat is tender. Serve with steamed rice or, even better, with pão or any dinner roll. This dish improves with time and can keep in the fridge for a week.

* You can find green chilies at any Indian grocery store. They're about the thickness of a pencil and about 1½–2 inches long.

** These are all dried red chilies readily available in India and many Indian markets. Kashmiris give color, Madras chilies give heat, and Bedkis give flavor. Kudos to you if you manage to find all three. If not, substitute what you can't find for other mild dried red chilies.

- **2½ lbs** pork shoulder, sliced into 1" cubes
- **1 recipe** *Marinade*
- **1 recipe** *Masala*
- **2 T** red wine vinegar
- **+** salt
- **+** steamed rice, pão, or dinner rolls for serving

Marinade

- **6** cloves
- **1 t** whole black peppercorns
- **2" stick** cinnamon, broken into pieces
- **½** star anise, broken
- **4–7** green chilies*, stems removed; sliced lengthwise
- **2" piece** ginger, peeled and crushed
- **15 cloves** garlic, peeled and crushed
- **2** medium onions, chopped into rough chunks
- **2 T** red wine vinegar
- **7** large Indian bay leaves (They're larger than Turkish bay leaves and have several large veins running lengthwise. If you can't find them, substitute regular bay leaves.)
- **2 T** coarse salt

Masala

- **1" piece** ginger, peeled and chopped roughly
- **8 cloves** garlic, peeled
- **1 onion,** chopped roughly
- **1 t** black peppercorns
- **7** cloves
- **½** star anise, broken
- **1½ T** whole coriander seeds
- **1 T** cumin seeds
- **1½ t** black mustard seeds
- **6** Madras chilies**
- **6** Kashmiri chilies**
- **6** Bedki chilies**
- **½ t** ground turmeric
- **1 golf-ball-size lump** tamarind paste

DHOL DHOL

Adapted from Ron Timmins | Makes 1 9" × 9" pan (36 small pieces)

When the British finally quit India in 1947, the remaining Anglo-Indian population (i.e., Brits born on Indian soil, and people of mixed English and Indian descent) was given the option to choose between British and Indian citizenship. Those who remained in India continued living in the major cities and administrative centers they had always called home—places like Calcutta, Madras, and Bombay, or old colonial hill stations like Ooty, Shillong, and Simla.

In Madras, the first permanent British settlement on the subcontinent and one of the oldest centers of Indian Christianity, dhol dhol has been an essential sweet for the Christmas feast for at least a century. Variations of the dish exist down India's western coast, many of them prepared using a combination of ordinary white rice flour and wheat flour. This Anglo-Indian version from Madras uses black rice, which originally came to India from Burma, and turns up in another dessert specialty in Chettinad, a region populated by wealthy Hindu traders to the southwest of Madras.

Ron Timmins, who showed me how to make a traditional dhol dhol, only knows this dish as a local holiday specialty among members of the Anglo-Indian community he was raised in. In the Madras of his childhood, Timmins remembers dhol dhol was cooked over wood flames, and the dense, sticky batter needed to be stirred for an hour or more. The recipe below uses a microwave to quarter the total cooking time and all but eliminate the totally exhausting stirring process, exactly the type of exigency one tends to adopt when no longer living in a place where domestic help is commonplace.

---

2 C black rice
1 14-oz can (~2 C) coconut cream (or substitute coconut milk)
1 C sugar
½ t salt
2 T ghee
+ unsalted butter

1 The day before preparing the dhol dhol, soak the rice for 8–10 hours, then strain and lay out on a baking sheet to dry overnight. The next day, grind the dry rice into a fine flour. A high-powered blender works best; otherwise, grind the rice in batches in a coffee grinder.

2 Mix the rice flour, coconut cream (or milk), sugar, and salt together in a large, microwave-safe bowl until you have a smooth, glossy batter with no lumps.

3 Once the batter is mixed, nuke it on high for 5 minutes. After 5 minutes, the batter will have firmed around the edges and remained liquid in the center. Remove from the microwave and stir to combine the two textures.

4 Return the bowl to the microwave and nuke for 5 more minutes. Remove from the microwave, add the ghee, and stir until incorporated. This will be a little difficult as the batter will have become a sticky mass at this point, almost the texture of taffy, and will form a dense loaf in the center of the bowl.

5 Once the ghee is incorporated, nuke the mixture for 5 more minutes. In the meantime, grease a 9-by-9-inch pan with butter. After 5 minutes, the mixture will come out bubbling vigorously. The mixture should now be extremely gummy and a deep, shiny purple, roughly the color of eggplant skin. Stir to incorporate the butter that has risen to the top.

6 Pour the mixture into the brownie pan—it should be about an inch thick—and smooth the top with the back of a knife. Sprinkle the surface with slivered almonds and gently press them in.

7 Before it's completely cool, cut the dhol dhol into 1½-inch squares. Store in a sealed container, separated with parchment paper, or wrap the pieces individually.

PUNJABI GOAT AND POTATO CURRY

Adapted from Bakshish Dean | Makes 6 servings

When we eat "Indian" food in the United States, what we're usually eating is Punjabi food, a cuisine rich in meat and dairy from one of the most prosperous and ancient regions of the subcontinent. Civilization first flourished here in the third millennium BC; since then, Punjab has seen an endless succession of rulers, faiths, and cultures. It's been controlled by Greek, Hindu, Buddhist, Islamic, Sikh, and, under the British, Christian rulers. Today, bisected by the Partition in 1947, the Punjab region is split between Pakistan and India. In Indian Punjab, Christians, largely converted by British missionaries in the late nineteenth century, represent roughly 1 percent of the population.

Because Christmas lunch in the Punjab tends to be a village-wide celebration involving people from different faiths, the use of goat meat keeps this dish from alienating anyone. According to the Punjabi Christian Delhi-based chef Bakshish Dean, the recipe below, with its roots in the region's Muslim culinary traditions, would typically be prepared in large quantities over an open fire and followed with sweets like *gujia*, a fried, crescent-shaped pastry dipped in simple syrup.

1 Use a mortar and pestle to pound the ginger, garlic, and green chilies into a rough pulp. Set aside.

2 Heat a heavy-bottomed pan over a medium flame. Add ghee and, once hot, add the whole spices (cardamom, cloves, cumin, bay, peppercorns, cinnamon). Fry for about 30 seconds before adding the sliced onion, meat, ginger-garlic-chili pulp, ground spices (coriander, turmeric, red chili powder, garam masala), and salt. Stir to distribute.

3 Cook over high heat, stirring often, for about 5–7 minutes, or until the mixture comes to a simmer. Reduce heat and cover, stirring every 10 minutes. After 20 minutes, add the quartered potatoes and cook for 10 more minutes.

4 Uncover, increase the heat to medium, and cook for 10 more minutes, stirring frequently, before adding the tomatoes. Cook for another 10 minutes or so.

5 At this point, you can choose to add up to 2 cups of water if you like a soupier curry, or leave as is for a thicker one. Simmer for 15 more minutes. The meat should be very tender. If not, continue to simmer. Remove from heat, check seasoning (you can add more garam masala), then scatter with cilantro. Serve with rice.

2" piece ginger, peeled and sliced
10 cloves garlic, peeled
6–8 Indian green chilies, roughly chopped (see note, page 139)
½ C ghee
4 pods black cardamom, lightly crushed
6 cloves
½ t cumin seeds
2–3 Indian bay leaves
¼ t whole black peppercorns
4" cinnamon stick, broken in half
2 small onions, sliced
2½ lbs goat meat (a mix of rib chops, lower saddle, and bone-in leg), cut into 2" pieces
2 t ground coriander
½ t ground turmeric
2 t red chili powder
½ t garam masala
+ salt (more to taste)
2–3 medium yellow potatoes, peeled and quartered
2 medium tomatoes, chopped
+ cilantro, roughly chopped

STICKY RICE CAKES

Adapted from Hoihnu Hauzel | Makes about 20 cakes

One of the defining features of northeastern cooking—particularly in the states sharing borders with Burma—is the use of sticky rice. These sticky rice cakes are a popular holiday snack (with a variety of names) for a number of regional hill tribes, including Nagas from Nagaland; Paites from Manipur; Mizos from Mizoram, once among India's most dangerous regions and now one of its most rapidly developing states; and Bodos, currently engaged in a long-standing and sometimes violent push for autonomy from the state of Assam. They're usually served with jaggery (raw cane sugar) and tea.

Though it's no longer difficult to come by sticky rice, the ingredient used to be a scarce commodity saved for special occasions, like Christmas, when rice cakes like these would be served as a rare treat during visits with family and friends.

This is an unusually tame dish from a region best known for its love of meat and fermentation. Hoihnu Hauzel, who works as a reporter for the *Times of India* and grew up in the northeastern corner of Manipur, shared his recipe with me.

5 C (about 2¼ lbs) sticky rice flour (also known as sweet rice flour)
1 t salt
5 T granulated sugar
2–3 C water
12 plantain or banana leaves, thawed if frozen
+ jaggery (raw cane sugar), honey, or maple syrup, for serving

1 Mix the sticky rice flour with salt and sugar. Add water gradually while stirring until you have a smooth, solid dough that holds its shape. It will look like cookie dough.

2 Form the dough into small cakes about ½-inch thick (2 or 3 tablespoons for each one), then wrap them like tamales in pieces of plantain or banana leaves—keep the ridged side of the leaf on the outside.

Tie the packets securely with string. Fill a large pot with water. Submerge the packets in the water, cover the pot, bring to a boil, and cook for about 15 minutes. Remove a packet from the water to check for doneness; the cake should have a smooth exterior and a sponge-like interior. If that's the case, pull the rest.

3 Serve with jaggery, honey, or maple syrup to be spooned onto the cakes.

SORPOTEL

Adapted from Mary Fernandes | Makes 6–8 servings

Sorpotel is prepared in some form or another practically every-where the Portuguese planted their flag. It appears among East Indian and Mangalorean communities in India, and in a blander guise in Brazil, where it's known as *sarapatel*. Among Goans, variations from household to household can be significant, with the mixture and proportion of spices and chilies changing pretty dramatically between versions of the *reshad* masala that gives the dish its flavor. In some regions, the meat is simply diced and cooked with masala, vinegar, and onions; in other versions, including this one, the meat is par-boiled, chopped, pan-fried, and finally stewed for more diversity of texture. Some sorpotels are an intimidating shade of red, others a more sedate brown. Some use pig's blood, either fresh or dry, which thickens the gravy and adds a complexity and tang.

What every sorpotel has in common is the mixture of pork, liver, and other offal; the offal that gets used in a family's sor-potel typically depends on how much the family can afford to spend. Liver is non-negotiable, but poorer families might sup-plement small quantities of costly meat with a wide variety of innards including lung, heart, kidney, and tripe. The version here belongs to Mary Fernandes, whose nephew Gresham, a well-known cook in Bombay, prepared it for me in my virtually counter-space-less seven-by-four-foot kitchen. It was a pre-Christmas miracle.

1 Place your pig ears and pork hock into one pot, and liver in another. To each pot, add enough water to cover by 1 inch, then add 1 table-spoon of vinegar, 1 teaspoon of turmeric, and a generous pinch of salt. Cook at a slow boil until the meat has become firm but not totally cooked, about 15–20 minutes, skimming the fatty yel-low scum that rises to the top with a spoon as you go.

2 Once the meat is par-boiled, remove it from the water and cool. (Reserve the ear-and-hock-boiling water; you'll use it later.) Chop all the meat into uniform ¼-inch cubes.

3 Heat 2 tablespoons oil in a saucepan and add the onions, cooking over low heat until they're caramelized. The sweetness from the onions will counteract the sourness of the masala, so make sure they're deep brown. Once cooked, add 2 tablespoons of the *masala* paste and stir in, then add about 1 cup of ear/hock stock and stir to combine. Turn off the heat and leave in the pan.

4 In another hot frying pan, brown the chopped meat in oil over high heat. You shouldn't need much oil, as the meat will render along the way. You can do this in batches if necessary to make sure every-thing is nicely browned. Once browned, transfer the meat to the pot with the onions and masala, straining out excess fat as you go. If the meat leaves a significant amount of fond in the pan, deglaze it with some of the ear/hock stock and add this to the meat-and-masala mixture.

5 Once all the meat is in the saucepan, turn the heat to medium and add another cup of stock and two tablespoons of masala paste. Bring to a low simmer and cook for about 45 minutes. In the end, you want a modest amount of medium-thick gravy. (Think the consistency of wet dog food—not an attractive image, but apt.) You may need to add up to

2 more cups of stock and 3 tablespoons of masala paste as the liquid reduces.

6 In the last couple of minutes, stir in the powdered blood and bring the mixture up to a boil for about a minute, stirring constantly to incorporate the blood, which will act as a thickener, then remove it from the heat. Check the flavor and add more salt and/or vinegar to taste. The vinegar flavor should be pronounced but not overwhelming.

7 You can eat this dish the same day, but traditionally, sorpotel is meant to be eaten on the third day. If you're fearless about food safety and want to do as real Goans do, here's how: leave the sorpotel on the stove half-covered overnight. When you wake up the next morning, bring it to a boil for 2–3 minutes, then leave it to sit for the day. In the evening, bring it to another boil for 2–3 minutes. (You'll need to add water or stock with each boil to keep the liquid content right.) At this point, you can refrigerate the sorpotel. The next day, bring it out, boil it once more, and eat it.

FOR THE MASALA

This is best made in bulk, but you'll rarely use more than a few tablespoons at a time. This recipe makes more than you need, but will keep for up to a year in the fridge. One particularly good option is to take whole mackerel, slather the insides with the masala, and fry them.

1 Roast the chilies in a dry pan over low heat until fragrant and toasty; set aside. Dry-roast the whole spices (cumin, cardamom, cinnamon, fenugreek, black mustard, cloves, black peppercorns).

2 Blend the roasted ingredients with the remaining reshad ingredients together in a blender or food processor until it's a thick, red paste, roughly the texture and color of tomato paste. If necessary, add up to ¼ cup of water to achieve the right texture.

- **2** pig ears (and/or kidneys, heart, lungs, or any other offal that strikes your fancy)
- **2½ lbs** pork hocks
- **1 lb** pork liver
- **2 T** red wine vinegar
- **1 t** turmeric
- **+** salt
- **+** vegetable oil
- **2** large onions, minced
- **~5 T** *Reshad Masala*
- **2 T** dried pig's blood, powdered (optional)*

Reshad masala
- **50** dried Kashmiri chilies (stems off and, if you like less spice, seeds removed)
- **1 T** cumin seed
- **2 pods** green cardamom
- **2" stick** cinnamon
- **½ t** fenugreek seeds
- **½ t** black mustard seeds
- **½ t** cloves
- **½ t** black peppercorns
- **½ C** red wine vinegar
- **1 T** turmeric
- **7 cloves** garlic, peeled
- **2" piece** ginger, peeled
- **1 t** sugar
- **½ C** cashew *feni* (a Goan cashew liquor; or substitute ¼ C white tequila)

* To powderize blood, purchase about ¼ lb coagulated blood, most readily available from Asian grocery stores or Chinatown butchers. Slice the blood as thin as you can and place the slices on a parchment paper–lined cookie sheet. Set your oven to the lowest setting and place the tray inside, leaving the door slightly ajar. It should take the blood about 8 hours to dry. It will shrink considerably and turn from a deep, almost-purple brown to a dark-coal black. When the pieces become brittle, break them into small shards, which you can then blitz to a fine powder in a good coffee grinder. Other communities that make sorpotel often omit the blood, which you can do, too, if drying blood does not sound like a fun way to spend an afternoon.

In the back kitchen of Jaaneman Sweet Centre, an Indian sweetshop in the London neighborhood of Arnos Grove, Nalim Bapodra stirred a pot of sugar syrup over a gas flame. It was the day after the Muslim holiday of Eid al-Fitr and Bapodra, the shop's owner, was out of almond *burfi*, a delectable fudge–like confection of boiled milk, sugar, and nuts.

Burfi is a subcategory of *mithai*, a family of sweets synonymous with celebration across the subcontinent. Mithai are enjoyed by everyone, regardless of religion or region. They're given as gifts, eaten at weddings, served on auspicious occasions of all sorts, and even offered to Hindu gods. I had arrived at Bapodra's shop with a stomach already full of sweets; in this case, beet *halwa*, a pudding–like treat that I'd eaten with *biryani* and chicken curry at my family's Eid party the night before.

Before I met my husband, I'd never tasted an Indian sweet. We both grew

MITHAI MASTER

BY **SARAH ELTON**   ILLUSTRATION BY **CELINE LOUP**

up in Toronto. A friend introduced us when we were in our twenties. He took me for the first time to Toronto's Gerrard Street East, the Indian strip where I tasted fresh *jalebis* and dense, fudgy milk cake, and we fell in love. He traces his roots back to the Indian state of Gujarat. Though it's been three generations since the family lived in India, their appreciation for mithai persists.

If you weren't raised in a South Asian home, you might not know a *ladoo* from a *chumchum*. Particularly if your experience with Indian cuisine is limited to the buffet, you might have only encountered canned *gulab jamun*, shipped from India, drowning in sugary syrup—not the best advertisement for the splendorous diversity of mithai. Without friends or relatives who take their sweets seriously, you might even have been disappointed by the burfi that's sold at south Asian groceries, which is usually dry yet simultaneously greasy. This is a shame.

Mithai are both multitudinous in their variety and vital in their ritual function. Desserts like rice pudding and the crispy, airy fried-dough squiggles called jalebi are enjoyed universally, while others carry more significance in particular traditions. For Muslims at Eid, it's customary to make a pudding called *seviyan* with thickened milk and fine vermicelli noodles.

Specific mithai are offered on various holidays to the different Hindu gods. For Ganesh Chaturthi, there are *modaks*, the elephant-God's favorite, a coconut-stuffed steamed dumpling made from cooked rice-flour dough. At Durga Puja, a coconut ball called *narkel naru* is blessed by the priest. Nothing is wasted—the sweets are always eaten after a ceremony. And everybody gives sweets as gifts. During the Hindu festival of Diwali, Bapodra, who is Hindu, sells as much as 300 kilos of *pedas* and about 140 large trays of burfi. His sweets are so sought after that a family living in Florida recently offered to pay his airfare and accommodations for a week to prepare sweets for a wedding.

In our family everyone says the best mithai come from London, specifically from Bapodra's shop. So when I turned up and he offered me a lesson, I jumped. "No book, no university, no college can teach you this," he said, smiling. "These are our five-thousand-year-old recipes. They've been passed down from generation to generation." Bapodra is in his sixties, his gray roots growing out under his dyed-black hair, but as he instructed me in mithai making, he exhibited the energy of an excited boy.

Bapodra knows his mithai. In India, Bapodra's parents provided milk for their village, selling what they took from three cows and four water buffalo. Bapodra would deliver it to customers on his bicycle, ladling out what they wanted that day from a big aluminum canister. What was left over wouldn't keep without refrigeration, so his mother made mithai for the family. (The history of mithai making is tied to the need to preserve fresh milk in a hot climate. Once you boil milk down, evaporating the water, it keeps longer.)

Bapodra learned to make mithai after immigrating to England from India. He'd come to work as an accountant but couldn't find a job, so his father-in-law taught him to make the sweets to sell. A photograph of Bapodra's father-in-law hangs above the counter in the shop; he had been head cook for a wealthy plantation owner in East Africa and kept all his recipes in his head, including those for dozens of mithai he made there.

In Bapodra's kitchen in London, the candy stove is set low to the ground for easy stirring with a large, oar-like spoon. "Hold it like this and you never tire," he said, tucking the long handle into his body. After the sugar syrup reached what he deemed to be the perfect thickness, he added cardamom. Then he poured hot milk over a basin filled with milk powder—a substitute for *mawa*, the traditional thickened-milk base for many mithai. (Bapodra tells me that in the West, commercially prepared mawa is made with added thickeners, so he avoids it.) He used his hands to mix the milk powder with the liquid. "In America, it is all hygienic, but it is best done by hand," he said. He combined the milk mixture with the sugar syrup, and made it my responsibility to stir it over the flame. After only a few minutes of stirring, it looked like polenta; as I continued, it became increasingly smooth. It was hot and tiring work.

"These days no one wants to work hard like us," Bapodra said. He's ready to retire, but those who are interested in buying his business don't want to learn how to make the sweets. They want him to stay on. His two children have chosen their own careers—his daughter trained in scriptwriting and his son designs video games. In India there are still many *halvais*—food artisans who make mithai for a living—but they don't get visas to work in the West. Nevertheless, people living here with roots in the subcontinent long for mithai, which are a connection to culture and to the past. Bapodra told me that when he eats a mithai, he thinks of his mother and his grandmother. "They always made the best mithai," he said. He doesn't sell his favorite one in the store, though, because he says that it's the one mithai people still make at home. It's called *magaj* and is made with chickpea flour, butter, sugar, nuts, and flavored with cardamom and saffron. "It's Lord Krishna's favorite," he said.

When the milk and sugar had cooked into a smooth, creamy batter, Bapodra added the almonds and then scooped it onto a well-greased tray. In a few hours, it would set into a thin, firm cake and get sliced into single-portion squares. When we finished, he told me the real secret for making his famous mithai: "Most importantly, you put in your effort and love," he said. "Always make mithai with your heart." LP

THERE ARE MANY, MANY VARIETIES OF MITHAI,

and recipes from different regions draw on the abundance of that particular place, from dairy to grains to legumes. The one quality all mithai have in common is that they are extremely sweet. —SARAH ELTON

LADOO

Ladoos are dense, round balls about the size of a doughnut hole that are made dozens of ways, using a wide range of ingredients, from fine ver-micelli noodles to chickpea flour. Take a bite and the ladoo might crumble; they can be dense and almost dry.

REGION: Gujarat, Rajasthan, Delhi
SIGNATURE INGREDIENT: cardamom
ALIASES: *laddoo, laddu*

JALEBI

Jalebis, eaten all over, are disks of crispy, deep-fried dough squiggles often colored bright orange and saturated in sugar syrup.

REGION: Punjab (via Iran)
SIGNATURE INGREDIENTS: saffron (or yellow food coloring), chickpea flour
ALIASES: *zulubiya, jilapi*

PEDA

Pedas are round, soft balls flavored with cardamom that taste a bit like caramel and are made by simmering—and simmering and simmering—milk and adding mawa. They're caramel colored here, but Bapodra says when you make pedas with buffalo milk, they're white.

REGION: Uttar Pradesh and Gujarat
SIGNATURE INGREDIENTS: mawa, car-damom, sometimes pistachios or almonds
ALIASES: *pera, penda, pendha*

MAWA

Mawa is the foundation for milk-based sweets. To make it, full-fat milk (buffalo or cow) is reduced to a thickened, creamy mass that starts to dry out and stick together and looks like a firm ball of mozzarella. But mawa can be denser and harder to grate than cheese; it is melted to be made into sweets like burfi.

REGION: Rajasthan
SIGNATURE INGREDIENT: fresh buffalo or cow milk
ALIASES: *khoya, khoa, mava*

ILLUSTRATIONS BY HELEN TSENG

RABRI

This rich, creamy dessert, reminiscent of custard, is basically a pudding made from the scum that forms on the top of milk when you cook it. The trick is to stir the milk as it boils, incorporating the thick skin that forms on top, until you have a smooth, thickened substance. You then add sugar and (optionally) rosewater, and garnish with thinly sliced pistachios and almonds. You'd never know it's just sweetened milk scum.

REGION: Uttar Pradesh and Punjab
SIGNATURE INGREDIENTS: milk, sometimes rose water
ALIAS: *rabdi*

SANDESH

In the eastern subcontinent, mithai are often made by curdling milk with an acid like lime juice, as if to make cheese. This is called *chhena,* or *paneer.* When you mix the white, creamy, plain-tasting cheese with sugar, corn flour, and cardamom, you have the base for Bengali treats like delicate, melt-in-your-mouth *sandesh* or spongy, even-sweeter *rasgulla,* served floating in sugar syrup.

REGION: Bengal
SIGNATURE INGREDIENTS: chhena, cardamom, corn flour
ALIAS: *pranhara*

CHUM CHUM

Chum chums are supersweet and eye-catching, as they're often colored bright pink and shaped into little logs. They're made with chhena and are moist and grainy.

REGION: Bengal and Uttar Pradesh
SIGNATURE INGREDIENT: chhena
ALIASES: *cham cham, chomchom*

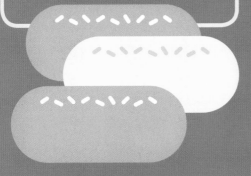

URADIA

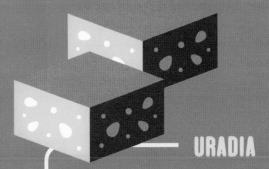

In the south, mithai are often built on fruit, chickpea flour, and lentils. *Uradia* are one such mithai, made with *urad* lentils. Bapodra shared some of his personal stash. He cut it into squares like a brownie. It was grassy from the lentils and crunchy from the sugar crystals he purposely didn't melt.

REGION: Andhra Pradesh
SIGNATURE INGREDIENT: black lentils
ALIASES: *urad dal ladoo, sunnundalu*

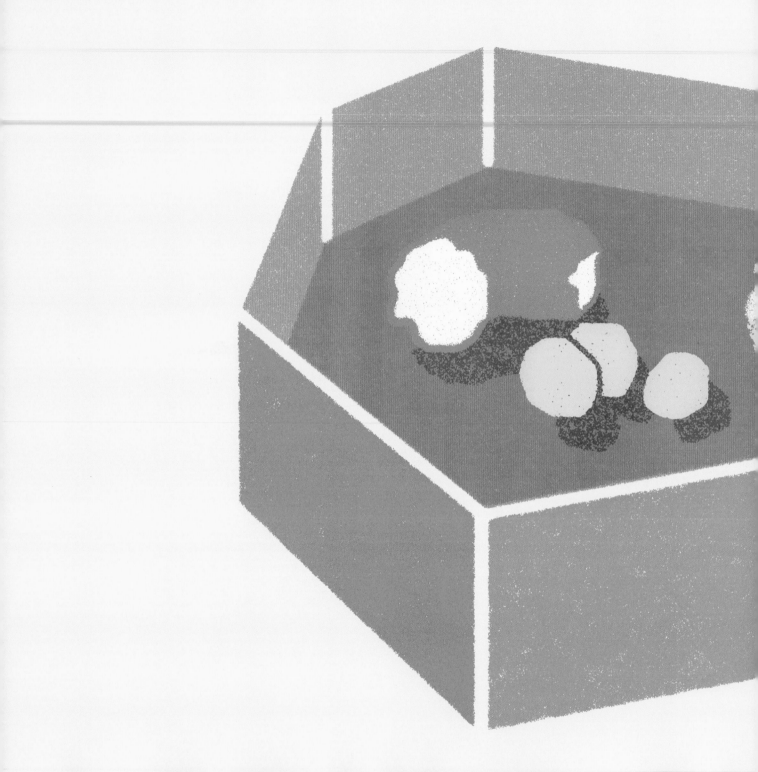

LOSING TH

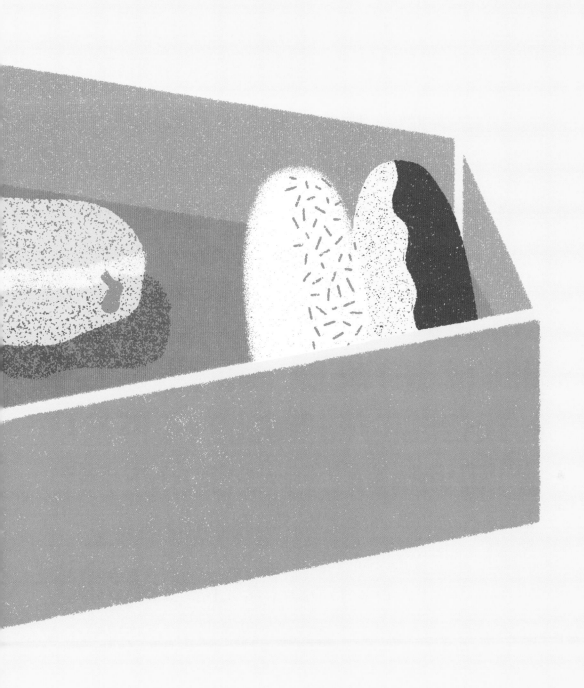

HE PLOT

JESSICA
LAMB-
SHAPIRO

WHEN I AGREED TO BE A PALLBEARER AT MY GRANDMOTHER'S FUNERAL, I HADN'T CONSIDERED HOW LARGE A CASKET REALLY IS, THE SIGNIFICANT WEIGHT OF WOOD, OR MY GENERAL INSUFFICIENCY IN MATTERS OF PHYSICAL STRENGTH. THE BEST I COULD HOPE FOR WAS TO BE SANDWICHED IN BETWEEN TWO BRAWNIER RELATIVES, THOUGH YOU WOULDN'T REALLY USE THE WORD *BRAWNY* TO DESCRIBE ANY OF THE SHAPIROS. I DECIDED I WOULD BRING EXTRA DIGNITY TO THE OCCASION, TO MAKE UP FOR MY LACK OF PHYSICAL STRENGTH. I WOULD OUT-SOLEMN EVERYONE. *PALLBEARER:* I TURNED THE WORD OVER AND AROUND IN MY MIND. I WOULD BEAR PALL LIKE NOBODY'S BUSINESS.

It was April, and it had been raining intermittently all day. When the hearse arrived at the ceremony, we six pallbearers lined up, three on each side, to receive the coffin. My mind flooded with questions. How would we carry it? Was it supposed to go on our shoulders?

My grandmother, born in 1920, died just days before her eighty-seventh birthday. She had not only lived a long life, but had survived several near-death hospitalizations. I remember being called down from college because she was in a coma. Almost as soon as I arrived, she woke up. "What is your name?" the doctor asked. "Frances Shapiro," she answered. "Who is the president of the United States?" he asked. "Bush," she said, "and I hate him."

Focusing on the task at hand was a way for me to avoid feeling. I missed my grandmother. The good-hearted grandmother is a cliché, but mine was preternaturally kind and almost pathologically incapable of saying a bad word about anyone (the Bush comment was an exception). My father and I used to hide rubber snakes in her bed, which wasn't very nice of us, but she never got angry about it. She had tolerated a lot in her life—most notably in her marriage, where my grandfather had a long and public affair with a friend of hers.

She wrote letters on personalized gold-embossed stationary, always sent thank-you notes, and was a voracious reader. She was my personal weatherman: no matter where I lived or how old I was, she'd call to warn me if snow or rain were coming, and to make sure I was wearing a jacket and hat.

As expected, my practical pall-bearing skills proved subpar. My hands were sweaty and slippery. The coffin, a giant pentagon shellacked into an unnatural shine, was bigger than I'd expected. When I absorbed the weight of it, my black heels sank ominously into the mud. I kept switching my grip, trying to find one that worked. We'd only gone a few feet when I heard a shrill, theatrical scream.

We stopped processioning. I couldn't see what had happened since my face was up against the coffin, blocking my view. My arms felt like they were going to separate from my shoulder sockets.

Someone shouted, "Turn around!" This was easier said than done. We had barely managed to walk in a straight line. Which way should we turn? Who would initiate the rotation? Do you mean your left or mine?

"Let's just walk backwards," said my cousin. We backwards-baby-stepped the coffin into the hearse. I wiped my raw, sweaty palms on my black dress. Truth be told, I was happy to get a break. I went to see what the problem was.

The term *grave cut* refers to the hole dug for a body's interment. Ideally, the grave cut is made in the exact spot where the deceased is to be buried. Ideally, the grave cut is in the correct plot. My grandmother, Frances Shapiro, born Frances Witt, was married to Theodore Shapiro, who died in 1979. He was buried in the Witt family plot, which my grandmother's father James Witt had purchased, and where he and my great-grandmother Dora were buried. My grandmother was to be buried in this plot with her parents, her brother Danny, who had died of cancer when he was only thirty-six, and next to her only husband, Theodore, who was called Teddy.

There was a grave cut for the casket next to a Theodore Shapiro, but not the same Theodore Shapiro my grandmother had been married to. My grandmother's younger sister Lillie was the source of the scream. Lillie adds a touch of drama to the most banal of interactions. I've always liked the way she speaks: everything she says is delivered like a line in a play, or like she is imparting an important secret. She doesn't say "hello"; she says, "Hello, daaaarling!" Lillie glowered at the rabbi. Moments earlier, we had looked to him to guide us; now he had led us to a spectacular slapstick. In everyday life, I expect a certain amount of benign pandemonium. But death rituals are choreographed and rehearsed. Funerals have few variations, which is part of why they are comforting. Now we were wildly off-script.

Sweating, the rabbi called someone on his cell phone. He suggested we try again tomorrow. My father said, "What are you going to do with my mother's body overnight?" Jewish custom dictates the deceased be buried within twenty-four hours. "Fix it," said my great-aunt Lillie to the rabbi in a tone that could not be argued with.

I was surprised and I wasn't surprised by the sudden bathos. Things like this happened in our family. My grandfather Teddy had been so dedicated a practical joker that I sometimes wondered if he was mentally ill. For two years, he pretended his car was a horse. He called it Betsy and attached ropes to the steering wheel. He used the ropes to steer the car. He regularly swapped a rubber chicken for my grandmother's roasted one. This kind of mishap would have delighted him. If I believed in ghosts, I'd think he was behind it.

It started to rain. I worried about the elderly relatives, who made up the primary demographic of the funeral party. Don't old people get pneumonia easily? There was a small structure with bathrooms that could have served as a shelter from the rain, but it was locked.

A half hour passed. My grandfather's brother, whom everyone called Uncle Abe, and who had a serious gambling problem and still owed my grandmother a significant amount of money, announced loudly that he needed the bathroom. Others joined this chorus. The rabbi found a key to the small building and we went inside. A long queue formed by the door of the bathroom, a queue that contained almost my entire family.

There is a minor disagreement between my father and me about what happened next, though we agree it was a moment of unexpected salvation. I remember the rabbi arriving with several pink and orange boxes of doughnuts from the Dunkin' Donuts across the street. My dad remembers it being one of the limo drivers.

Regardless of who brought them, the appearance of doughnut boxes immediately transformed the mood of our irritated and confused party. Suddenly, there was delight. Elderly relatives rushed to the doughnut boxes in a manner neither dignified nor safe.

There is no word for the role that food plays in post-funeral services, though there should be. It's always present. Food seems to be one thing that people reliably turn to for comfort. We need food to live; food reassures us that we are still alive. Just as a cake can celebrate a birthday, it can also serve as a manic defense against death. Sugar, in particular, activates the neural pathways that release dopamine. The old Dunkin' Donuts slogan—"Donuts, making people happy since 1950"—proves physiologically true. Yet it's rare that food appears *during* the funeral. I've never seen a graveside mourner enjoying a snack.

My boyfriend, David, and I were the last to reach the doughnuts. Pieces of fried dough, thoroughly mauled, lay trampled and torn at the table's perimeter, as though they had tried and failed to escape the massacre. Only one jelly–filled doughnut remained intact.

I abhor filled doughnuts. I hate surprises. I like to see what I'm eating before I eat it. I have a near-moral objection to the hiding of soft, mushy,

creamy surprises inside of a pastry. The insides squirt and gush out. The whole thing feels like chaos.

"You take it," I said to David.

The sun had come out, so we walked outside. There was nowhere to sit except on gravestones.

"This feels wrong," said David, sitting on a grave, eating his jelly doughnut. I agreed. The subtext seemed like: we are still alive, and now we are flaunting it.

Almost as strange as finding out the cemetery had accidentally dug the wrong grave cut was the hour or two my family spent hanging out in the cemetery, eating doughnuts. It was as though we were actors on a movie set, playing the part of mourners until someone yelled *cut* and we broke for lunch. There we sat, in our mourning costumes, neglecting our sadness—a moment out of time. We put our feelings and our sense of purpose on hold. What's odd is how completely capable we were of doing so.

I had not yet reached an age where the death of another made me reflect on my own death, though in some ways, I had carried a knowledge of death since I was a small child. My mother killed herself in 1979, just before my second birthday. I knew about death, I believed, and that knowledge made me different from other kids.

But that was all I knew about my mother. I wasn't taken to her funeral. I never visited her gravesite. I never asked about her. No one told me not to ask questions, but I imitated what I saw. Perhaps if I had been a bolder sort of child, my family in turn would have been more forthcoming. Perhaps if we had talked about her death more often, we would have visited her grave. And if we had visited her grave, even just once, I would have known *in advance* that she was buried here, in this cemetery.

But the morbid surprises, it turned out, were not done for the day. As

we waited for a backhoe to arrive, I walked with my father and aunt to the Witt family plot.

There was a sharp intake of breath, a moment of realization, of reckoning, then we all stopped breathing. I looked at the ground so I didn't have to look at anyone's face. I didn't know much about my mother, but I recognized her name when I saw it etched in stone: ELLEN RAPAPORT SHAPIRO, BELOVED WIFE AND MOTHER, BORN 1948, DIED 1979.

Death is hard to talk about; suicide, even harder. Think of how many terms there are for death—*crossing over, passing, dying, expiring, kicking the bucket*—and then think of how few there are for suicide: *killed herself, committed suicide, took her own life*. There are far more words for things in cemeteries than there are for suicide. A *cortege* is the funeral procession following the hearse. A *barrow* is a pile of stones placed on an otherwise unmarked gravesite. A *sepulchre* is a tomb carved into a hillside.

Even using the word *mother* is strange to me. I'm doing it for your benefit because it's a relationship I think you'll understand. But I don't understand it. I haven't come up with a phrase that I can use to refer to her that properly reflects the relationship. *Ellen* was her name, but that seems too impersonal for the person who gave birth to me. *Mother* sounds untrue because it connotes so much that never happened. *Birth mother* is accurate, but people mean something else when they say that. It's a linguistic problem as well as an emotional one. We have language to describe the things we want to communicate. A lack of language suggests something we can't see or don't want to see. It's hard to tell the difference.

Staring at the gravestone, I remained frozen on the outside. Inside, my atoms were agitating. Up until this moment, my mother was abstract, unreal, an idea. Under this stone were the bones of someone who was once a person. A

person with a body that gave birth to me. I felt like a weight was pulling me down toward the grave. I wanted to touch it. I wanted to dig into the earth and pull her bones out and hold them. To feel something solid, something that couldn't be ignored. *See?* I would say to my family, who preferred to pretend she had never existed. *Bones*.

We're fascinated by bones because they last so long. They tell us about a history we no longer have access to. There are no more mastodons, but scientists can reconstruct their skeletons and we can imagine what they looked like. It's evidence of something real, something we can see and touch. It's proof.

Without proof, it's all just stories. In a family, anyone can control a narrative. An absence of narrative is still a narrative. Not making a choice is still a choice. I wonder why we avoided this particular narrative as though our lives depended on it. I wonder why we tried so hard not to be human.

When I agreed to be a pall-bearer at my grandmother's funeral, I had not considered what it really means to "bear pall." A pall is a piece of cloth, usually white, black, or purple velvet, spread over a coffin. Figuratively, it has come to mean being enveloped in an atmosphere of gloom or despondency. The bearer is one who carries or brings or conveys; one who supports or sustains a weight, who holds up what would fall. My mother's suicide was a pall spread over my father and me; we had to bear it. But is *bearing it* simply surviving? Moving on—or as people who write about grief prefer to say—moving *through*? Or is it more like bearing witness?

I'm worried about how self-righteous it is to put myself in the role of *the one who conveys*. I've set up a dichotomy between silence and truth that is too tidy. I understand why no one wanted to talk about my mother's suicide. No one ever wants to talk about suicide. I don't even want to talk about suicide. I can be as lazy and ill-equipped and hypocritical and sadness-avoiding as anyone. The first thing I ever wrote about my mother's death was an incomprehensible one-act play, a string of nonsense words recited by actors. You wouldn't have known what it was about unless you were inside my brain. There were no complete sentences. There was no plot. I have a sentimental fondess for it now, like for a child's drawing of angry scratches labeled DOG. The way I used language both to express my story and, at the same time, to bury it completely.

Once the correct grave had been dug, we, the pallbearers, carried the casket over. We placed it on the bier as gracefully as we could. As I stepped away from the casket, I noticed that the pile of dirt from the new grave cut had been placed on top of my mother's headstone. It was a large pile of dirt, six feet worth. Her grave was buried. I couldn't help but think that if the wrong cut had not been dug, this pile of earth would have been here when we arrived. I wouldn't have seen my mother's grave, and no one would have remembered to mention it or remembered it was there at all. I don't really believe there's a being or a controlling force in the universe that interferes with our lives, orchestrates what we perceive as mistakes or successes, and secretly guides what happens to us. But if such a thing did exist, and if it had a penchant for grand gestures, you couldn't ask for something more pointed than this. It almost bothers me, how perfect it seems. **LP**

MILE END DOUGHNUTS

MAKES ABOUT 24 DOUGHNUTS

These doughnuts from Mile End Deli in New York City aren't the cakey, iced-and-sprinkled rings most people think of when they hear *doughnuts*. Instead, they're ethereal puffs, like fried custard, that are rolled in cinnamon sugar then doused with chocolate.

Whereas traditional Hanukkah doughnuts (*sufganiyot*) are jelly filled, these call for a sauce made of chocolate and Cardamaro, a thistle-based amaro. Eli Sussman, the chef de cuisine of Mile End, likes the earthy, vegetal taste it brings to the chocolate, which cuts the fat in the way that drinking Fernet does.

The doughnuts are made from a loose batter, and there's no kneading or shaping required—just stirring, waiting, and frying. Dusted in cinnamon sugar right out of the fryer, they're a dessert worthy of all the Judah-the-Maccabee, oil-burning-for-eight-days-instead-of-one Hanukkah celebrations you may have, or any lulls during a funeral. **—BRETTE WARSHAW**

1 In a large bowl, mix the flour, baking powder, salt, and 1 cup sugar.

2 In a second large bowl, whisk the eggs, vanilla bean innards, vanilla extract, and almond extract.

3 Whip the cream cheese in a stand mixer until fluffy, around 1 minute.

4 Add the cream cheese to the egg mixture and whisk well to combine.

5 Add the egg–cream cheese mixture to the dry ingredients. Whisk until completely combined. Cover and refrigerate for at least 3 hours.

6 Make the Chocolate-Cardamaro Ganache. Melt the chocolate in a double boiler. Once entirely melted, whisk in the powdered sugar.

7 Meanwhile, heat the heavy cream in a saucepan until warm but not simmering. Add the cream to the chocolate and whisk well. If the chocolate starts to seize, put it back over the double boiler for a few seconds, and then take it off again, continuing to whisk until smooth.

8 Add the vanilla extract and the Cardamaro to the chocolate mixture and whisk well. Keep warm.

9 Combine the remaining ½ cup sugar and cinnamon in a large bowl.

10 Heat your fryer oil to 350°F. Retrieve the batter from the fridge, and carefully scoop golf ball–sized rounds into the oil. Deep-fry for 6–7 minutes, until golden brown and just cooked through.

11 Remove the doughnuts from the fryer with a slotted spoon or strainer and immediately toss with the cinnamon sugar. Serve warm, with the Chocolate-Cardamaro Ganache.

INGREDIENTS

2½ C all-purpose flour
2 T baking powder
2 t salt
1½ C sugar
11 eggs
2 vanilla beans, scraped

2 T vanilla extract
1 t almond extract
2 C cream cheese, softened
+ Chocolate-Cardamaro Ganache
¼ C ground cinnamon
+ grapeseed oil, for frying

CHOCOLATE-CARDAMARO GANACHE

10 oz semisweet chocolate
½ C powdered sugar, sifted
1 C heavy cream
1 t vanilla extract
2 T Cardamaro

PHOTOGRAPH BY GABRIELE STABILE

BONE APPÉTIT

Brad Thomas Parsons

I was born in Central New York, smack in the middle of the state in Oneida, right off the New York State Thruway between Utica and Syracuse, and home to a distinct local fare. From the western side of the Thruway border comes salt potatoes, the summertime staple of baby potatoes boiled with a couple of handfuls of salt until the water evaporates, leaving the skins crusty and ghostly white. On the Eastern side of I-90, Italian red-sauce restaurants almost ubiquitously feature Utica greens, a concoction of garlicky escarole studded with prosciutto and pickled cherry peppers and topped with parmesan cheese. And for the holidays, from Thanksgiving through Christmas, gas stations, supermarkets, and specialty gift shops around the area stock up on jars of the local confection known as Turkey Joints.

Do you smoke them? That's the first question I get when I'm trying to turn someone new onto Turkey Joints. The next question: *Is there meat in them?*

Neither fowl nor narcotic, a Turkey Joint is a six-inch-long, knobby stick of candy-coated chocolate that resembles a turkey leg picked clean of meat. The candy shell has a shiny, pearl-colored lacquer with a shattering, ribbon-candy crunch that gives way to a Brazil nut–studded milk chocolate "marrow" inside. They're super sweet and best savored one or two at a sitting, rather than double-fisted like a bag of peanut M&M's.

Turkey Joints—originally called Turkey Bones—have been handmade the same way since 1919. They come from Nora's Candy Shop in Rome, NY, a small building on a residential street, nondescript but for a simple neon green sign promising TURKEY JOINTS. There, they're sold by the dozen in twelve-ounce glass jars, adorned with an emerald-green label with gold lettering and a logo flanked by two turkeys.

Turkey Joints have been a part of my Christmas morning since I was ten years old. My mother started the tradition, making sure a ribbon-topped jar of Joints was the centerpiece of the elaborate, customized baskets she put together for each of her kids. (A Christmas stocking would have split at the seams trying to hold in all the loot.) Each family member took a turn unpacking his or her basket, which overflowed with packs of gum, candy bars, scented candles, an annual Christmas ornament, jars of local honey, apple butter, maple syrup, bright orange clementines, and always a new toothbrush. Usually someone would immediately crack open the jar and crunch on the first Turkey Joint of the season, but I was more of a hoarder, rationing them out through New Year's Day.

On a Christmas morning about five years ago, there were no Turkey Joints under the tree. All day, we waited for the big reveal, playfully teasing my mother about the Year Without Turkey Joints. She laughed it off, but this turned out to be another sign—along with forgetting where she parked the car and missing appointments—of something more than simple forgetfulness. Soon after that Christmas, she was diagnosed with Alzheimer's; today, I don't think she knows what Turkey Joints are. For the past few years my sister Victoria has taken over the role of Turkey Joints provider. Turkey Joints have become a part of her teenage son Jack's Christmas mornings and now, even though I'm north of forty, she makes sure there's a green-and-gold jar with my name on it Christmas morning. Someday, I'll share this holiday tradition with my own family. Until then, I feel pretty lucky to have a jar each year to call my own. **LP**

(If you can't stop by the shop, you can order Turkey Joints online at *turkeyjoints.com*. They'll ship you a jar in the cooler months of the year, from October through May, for $19.99, though the shipping fee can climb to nearly the price of the candy itself.)

ORIGINAL CANDY
TURKEY
JOINTS
Since 1919

INGREDIENTS: BRAZIL NUTS, MILK CHOCOLATE,
MILK, COCOA BUTTER, CHOCOLATE LIQUOR, SOY
LECITHIN - AN EMULSIFIER, VANILLA - AN ARTIFICIAL
FLAVOR), SUGAR, CREAM OF TARTAR.
MAY CONTAIN: PEANUTS, TREE NUTS, EGGS, SOYBEANS

MANUFACTURED AT
NORA'S CANDY SHOP
321 N. DOXTATOR AVE · ROME, N.Y. 13440
(315) 337-4530 · FAX (315) 339-1054
www.turkeyjoints.com

NET WT. 12 oz.

0 15473 00001 3

The highly anticipated debut by Christian F. Puglisi

"With this book, Christian Puglisi demonstrates why he's one of the most influential contemporary chefs in the world. Since Relæ's inception, we've seen his ideas and aesthetics emulated in kitchens from New York to the very north of Sweden. Now we have the definitive document of his accomplishments, a book that shares his modern, daring, and singular concepts. An instant classic—and, dare I say, a masterpiece." ●●●●●●●○○●

—René Redzepi, chef of Noma and author of *René Redzepi: A Work in Progress*

1Ⓢ TEN SPEED PRESS

Christmas Dinner

PLEASE, THERE IS NO NEED TO "CHECK IN" ON ME. EVERYTHING IS FINE. WE'RE ALL GOOD NOW

MY DAD FOUGHT MY UNCLE. I GUESS THAT KICKED IT OFF

IT WAS FUNNY TO SEE THEIR TWO BODIES SPLAYED ACROSS THE DINING ROOM TABLE. WELL, SORT OF FUNNY. MY MOM AND AUNT REALLY FREAKED OUT. THEY WERE CRYING

MY NEPHEWS WERE CRYING. THEY NEED TO GROW UP. THEY ARE RECENT TEENAGERS - WHICH IS, LIKE, A HALFWAY ADULT

"I'LL GIVE YOU SOMETHING TO CRY ABOUT," I SAID, AS A LESS-RECENT TEENAGER

I WASN'T CLEAR ABOUT HOW THE FIGHT STARTED. SOMETHING ABOUT SOMETHING GOING DOWN DURING THE "SUMMER OF LOVE"

I TORE OFF A DRUMSTICK AND STRUCK MY GRANDFATHER ACROSS THE FACE WITH IT

BY MICHAEL DeFORGE

I HAD EVERY RIGHT TO BE UPSET. IT WAS MY ONE WEEKEND BACK AND THEY WERE FUCKING IT UP FOR ME. THEY COULDN'T EVEN HOLD IT TOGETHER FOR 72 HOURS

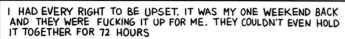

I STUCK A DOG IN THE MASHED POTATOES. SOME AUNT HAD SOME COUSIN IN A HEADLOCK. SHE FORCE-FED HIM GREEN BEANS UNTIL MY DAD SMASHED A CHAIR ON HIS HEAD

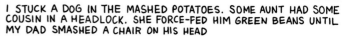

A COP CAME. HE WAS THE SAME ONE WHO HELPED HAUL ME OFF TO BEGIN WITH. HE HELD DOWN MY LEGS WHILE MY PARENTS TRIED TO GET ME IN THE CAR. I WOULDN'T GO VOLUNTARILY

BECAUSE WHO THE HELL "COOPERATES" IN THIS DAY AND AGE? IGNORANT PEOPLE, THAT'S WHO

WE SHOVED A PIECE OF PIE IN HIS MOUTH, HELD HIM DOWN, TORE OPEN HIS SHIRT AND FILLED IT WITH STUFFING

I WAS THROWING AS MUCH FOOD AROUND AS EVERYONE ELSE. I MEAN, I WAS ALREADY *THERE*, MAY AS WELL MAKE THE BEST OF IT

"WHEN IN ROME"

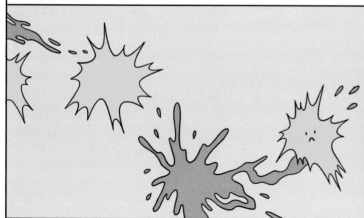

MY SISTER AND I TOSSED THE COP OUTSIDE, IN THE SNOW, AND POURED HOT GRAVY ON HIM. MY GRANDMOTHER WAS LATE. HER CAR SWERVED ONTO THE LAWN AND RAN OVER MY SISTER. SHE GOT BACK UP AND THEY STARTED WRESTLING

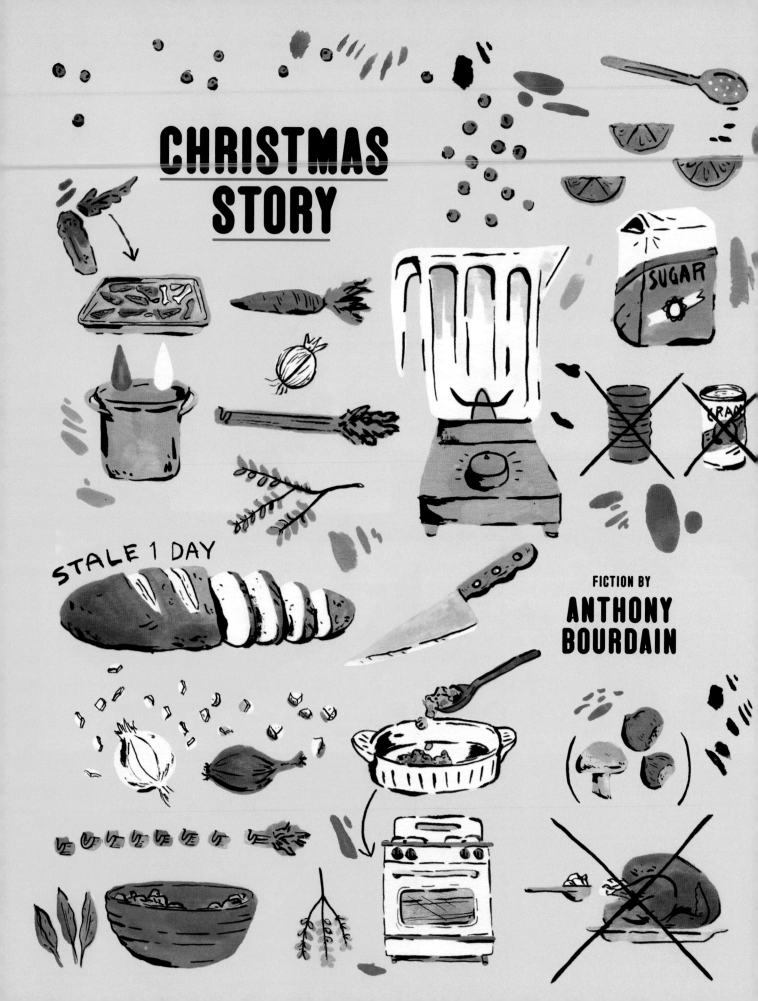

CHRISTMAS STORY

STALE 1 DAY

FICTION BY
ANTHONY BOURDAIN

2×

+

ILLUSTRATIONS BY
CARI VANDER YACHT

1

2

ALSO

R icky had been hacking around the restaurant business for twenty years when he took me under his wing. He'd never given much of a shit about the food, but he could talk a good game if called upon to do so. Which is how he must have scored the executive-chef gig at Villa Roma, a mammoth supper club, nightclub, and catering hall out on the Island.

He was one of these guys you'd find all the time in kitchens back in those days—the days before CIA and J&W and a thousand other Institutes of the Arts started spitting out company-sized units of culinary graduates every ten minutes, flooding the industry with bright young things with shiny new knife roll-ups and high expectations. Ricky was old school. Like a lot of his peers of the time, he'd rolled out of the military with some cooking experience, taken a job running one kind of kitchen or another, drunk and fucked his paycheck away for a decade or so, then—out of inertia, or just because the idea of re-engaging with the real world was too terrifying—ended up sticking with it.

He'd been bouncing from place to place for years, working bars, fish houses, short order, the occasional country club—stepping down from the chef's job and faking it as a line cook in fine dining when the situation required. He was what you'd call "solid": he showed up on time, quit drinking (much) and stealing (much), and was a good dad figure to whichever crew of knuckleheads he had to work with at the moment.

He lived alone in a rented apartment over a garage somewhere in Long Beach, had an ex-wife and a kid he never talked about. Outside of work he spoke of few interests other than the Mets, the Islanders, and Springsteen, of whom he was a devotee. "The Boss" could do no wrong in Ricky's book. It wasn't worth discussing. So I didn't.

Ricky had been put on this planet to do *volume*. It was his particular genius, his calling. Though he would have greatly preferred, he said, to play rhythm guitar professionally or make handcrafted furniture, what he was good at—no, brilliant at—was looking out at a banquet hall filled with five hundred people and knowing immediately, before even they knew, how many of them would go for the chicken and how many would break for the salmon.

He would slip through the kitchen doors, peek down over the balustrade, and return immediately to declare, "Golfers. Motherfuckers gonna hit the shrimp hard. Pull another twenty pounds outta the freezer now and run 'em under water. These people ain't gonna fill up on salad."

Other times he'd just have a sixth sense that what the people wanted, what they needed, was not the smoked salmon on cucumber rounds with paddlefish caviar that the client had ordered for them, or the Belgian endive leaves with tiny mounds of curried chicken salad and mango chutney—but what nobody had asked for: the Durkee frozen pigs in blankets, of which he kept a dozen cases in the freezer as emergency crowd-pleasers.

"You know what these cocksuckers want?" he'd muse, peering down at the heaving masses below. "Fucking sausages wrapped in pancakes."

He was never wrong.

He could see into the human heart.

Naturally, the holiday season was our busiest time. Every day from the beginning of December to the first week of January, we would do two, three office parties, special events: whole roasted tenderloins, baked hams, poached salmons in aspic, and, of course, turkeys. So many turkeys, the convection ovens looked like bowling-alley shelves—thirty, forty turkeys a day, barely out of their wrapping, still semifrozen. In the door, out of the box, into the ovens, and onto the buffet stations, sliced up and layered into hotel pans where they'd overcook under thick gravy heated over cans of flickering Sterno, or broken up into equitably divided portion-control parcels: a couple of generous-seeming-but-thin slices of white meat, over an equal amount of dark meat, over an ice cream scoop of stuffing, slapped on a plate, and sauced from a repurposed coffeepot. The necks, carcasses, and wing tips went into massive steam kettles, where they'd simmer pretty much constantly through the month.

My second year at the club, Ricky rewarded me for my yeoman-like work on the salad station all year by giving me Christmas Day off. This was an unheard-of windfall of free time, and at first I didn't know what to do with myself. I was still married then, and my wife was overjoyed. She had the idea to invite the families over for turkey fucking dinner with all the trimmings. "It'll be great," she said, lighting her fourth joint of the day. "It'll be, I don't know, so *normal!*"

What could I say? Not for nothing, but she had a point. I hadn't had a Christmas dinner or a holiday meal since I'd left home at seventeen. Since then, Christmases and New Year's Eves—even after service—were always and inevitably spent standing around the dish pit drinking Long Island iced teas, telling dick jokes with a bunch of cooks. She'd caught me at that point in a man's life where he starts to get reflective. I was wondering what it might be like to have a meal at a big table with normal people, with people who weren't cooks. The eggnog and the mistletoe and shit—it was starting to sound intriguing,

especially with Ricky's negative example looming so large. I didn't want to end up living over a garage, eating takeout and jacking off to the Spice Channel.

So I grabbed the chance gratefully, accepted the challenge, and invited everybody to dinner at my apartment: my mom and dad, my brother and his family, my wife's parents, and my sister and brother-in-law.

Here's the thing, though: five hundred people coming to Villa Roma I could do standing on my head, ice running through my veins. Two cases or three cases of pigs in blankets, it's all the same. You overproduce and you just roll the leftovers into the next party, because there is always a next party.

But at home? My ramshackle, broke-ass, paint-peeling, rent-stabilized apartment in Washington Heights? Ten people coming to dinner? This was deeply terrifying.

So I asked Ricky for advice.

"First thing you gotta know about Christmas is, you do *everything* in advance. Everything. Like, day before. Everything but the turkey," he said.

He was sitting behind his desk in the small office he shared with the steward, fiddling with an unlit cigarette he couldn't smoke indoors but planned to ignite on the loading dock shortly.

"Second thing you gotta know is that the murder rate spikes like crazy over Christmas—like doubles, *triples*! We're talking family on family! Brother against brother! Son against father! In-laws hacking each other with carving knives, Gramps taking a stab at Junior with the meat fork. It can get bad! Ask any cop." He was building steam. "And you know why? Not enough turkey. Or not enough of the piece somebody wants. Sure, there may be long, slow-cooking family disputes at work sometimes, some old grievance eating at one guy or another that kinda simmers away. But what sets 'em off every time? Somebody doesn't get the white meat they was expecting. Or the wing or the pope's nose, whatever. One second it's 'I love you, Unkie Paul,' next thing you know, it's 'Where's my fucking wing, cocksucker?! You ruined my life!'"

Ricky whistled through his teeth and reflected on something far away and somewhere over my head, as if he himself had been a veteran of many such blood fests.

"Sure," he continued, "when Dad comes across the table at Mom, starts gouging her eyeballs outta her skull in front of the whole family, shrieking 'You whore, you ruined my life!' there's for sure some history there. But it *starts*, believe me, with the turkey. So, remember. You gotta have enough turkey—of every part of the turkey. Or there's no telling what can happen. You see what I'm sayin'?"

I assured Ricky that I did.

"Okay, then. So. Let's start at the beginning: the cranberry relish. You can make that two, three days in advance. It only gets better. Unless you want that shit in the can, slides right out with the rings on it? You don't want that, do you? No sentimental attachment there? Okay. 'Cause some people do. Easy. You throw a bunch of cranberries in your food processor, some chunks of orange—with the peel still on, everything. Pulse. Throw in a buncha sugar, depending on how sweet you like it. Keeps for ages.

"Next thing you gotta think about is the gravy. Everybody fucks that up. They think, All I gotta do is, like, use the drippings in the pan. No. That's not how it works. You know this."

Ricky closed the door, settled in, and lit the cigarette. He'd have to put up with some shit from the steward later, and might have to stand up to some griping from the GM if the stew ratted him out, but he was clearly warming to his subject, boiling down a lifetime of making Christmas dinners for people.

"You have to look at it like this: The turkey, how many do you need? How many people you got coming over?"

"Twelve, counting me," I said.

"Okay. So you *think* you need one eighteen-pound bird, right? You're thinking a pound and a half per person, minus the bone, is maybe four to six ounces of meat. Load 'em up with the stuffing, the creamed pearl onions, brussels sprouts, your candied yams, and done, right?"

He took a deep drag on his cigarette and field-stripped it into a shellfish tag, crumpled it, and threw it in the trash.

"Wrong. You need *two* birds. And some assorted necks, backs, wings, whatever—for the stock. I know that seems like a lot, but worst thing that can happen is you got leftovers—and why the fuck does anybody even bother with Christmas if it isn't for the fucking leftovers? That's the best part. Next day. Asshole family's gone home, and it's just you sittin' on the couch, smokin' a nice fatty in front of the tube, about to tuck into a nice turkey sandwich. So, look:

day before the big event, you take out all the giblets and neck and shit. You take off the wing tips. The giblets and guts you save for later, of course. You're gonna put that in the gravy. But for now, you roast all those extra bones and the necks and wing tips, whatever, in a roasting pan. And when they're nice and brown, you deglaze the motherfucker, pour all that into a big stockpot, add cold water and your usual suspects—onion, carrot, celery, some sprigs of thyme—and simmer low and slow.

"Now you can start your stuffing. If you was smart, you already pulled a bunch of sliced bread to get stale. You dice all of that shit up, throw it in a big bowl. Fine dice onions, celery, shallots, and sauté that with some sage and some thyme. Maybe you want to throw in some roasted chestnuts, some mushrooms, depending how fancy you wanna get. Point is: you do *not* actually put the stuffing in the bird."

"Why not?" I asked, ignorant of the ways of the world.

"Turkeys are stupid," Ricky said. "Dumbest fucking creatures that ever lived. They're also not the cleanest creatures ever lived. You can wash the insides of a turkey all you want, there's still the possibility of salmonella or bacteria or some shit in there. Now, you jam an eighteen-pound turkey full of stuffing and roast it in a 375-degree oven long enough for it to get hot enough inside the center of the stuffing to kill all that bad shit? The outside—the meat on the breast and the leg—is gonna be cooked to shit. And for most of that cooking time, while you're waiting and hoping for the stuffing to cook, it's actually a nice, blood-warm temperature—the kind bacterias like a real lot. It gets 'em excited, makes 'em want to start fucking and multiplying and shitting all over themselves, and then there's something called 'log phase,' which is where there's so many bacterias in there they start dying off and what you have is bacteria bodies stacking up and that shit makes you sick, too."

I couldn't vouch for Ricky's authority on the subject of microbiology, much less his expertise on bacterial life span in a poultry environment, but I knew he'd taken the food-handling course.

"Point is," Ricky said, "you cook the stuffing on the side. You want to put stuffing inside your stunt turkey? Fine. As long as it's small. You roast an eighteen pounder—which is your business turkey—and your stuffing you pack into a separate roasting pan. You soak it with all the juice and fat that comes outta your roasting turkeys. The *other* turkey—a smaller one, maybe ten to twelve pounds—you can stuff that. That one's your stunt turkey. For show. Here's how it works:

"You roast both turkeys. The show turkey, the smaller one with the stuffing inside—you can even do that ahead of time if you don't have room in your oven. You bring that out to the table on a platter—*ta-da!*—and everybody goes 'oohh' and 'ahh' and 'ain't you a fucking genius' and then you whisk that fucker back into the kitchen where you have your eighteen pounder already broken down off the carcass. You got your breasts neatly removed, your legs off, wings good to go. You make a nice pile of hot stuffing in the center of the platter, you slice some dark meat around, crisscross your drumsticks and your wings, then you slice the breasts really pretty and shingle 'em back like dominoes leaning up the hill just right, and you bring that out like you just now broke down that whole bird, and there you go. Perfect family fucking Christmas. And nobody gets hurt."

I looked across the desk at my chef, my mentor, this man who had taught me so much over the years, and recognized the wisdom of his ways.

And then I went home and did exactly what he said.

Disaster was averted. There was happiness in the land. My family managed to get through the holidays without incident or recriminations. Everybody got enough white meat, and the next morning, sitting there on the couch by myself, I smoked a nice fatty and had a nice sandwich: thick slices of turkey, a wad of stuffing, a thin smear of cranberry, and some mayo. It was delicious.

Ricky was killed a few years later. He pulled over on the Taconic Parkway to help a stranded motorist in the snow and got hit by a passing minivan. He was a humanitarian to the end.

My wife ended up divorcing me. I probably should have told you that at the start. Christmas dinner might have gone okay, but it turned out she'd been banging her yoga instructor all along. I shouldn't have been surprised, but I was. Like Ricky, I just didn't see it coming. LP

chubo

CURATOR OF THE FINEST
JAPANESE KITCHENWARE

Focusing on performance, quality and precision, we've travelled throughout Japan to bring you the finest chef's knives and culinary tools.

View the collection at **chuboknives.com**

Sakai Takayuki • Takeda • Takamura • Saji Takeshi • Misono • Masahiro • Masamoto • Kanetsune • Glestain • Tojiro

CONTRIBUTORS

CHRISTINA AGAPAKIS is a biologist, designer, and science writer. She makes art with microbes, soil, and food.

JOSEPH AZAM lives in New York, where he practices law and lamb whispering. His writing has appeared in the *San Francisco Chronicle* and countless emails.

LIZ BARCLAY is a photographer in NYC and relocated Southerner. She is a lover of frozen negronis.

RAYMOND BIESINGER is a Montreal-based illustrator whose work has appeared in everything from awful photocopied zines to the *New Yorker*. Chief among his talents is the ability to defer lunch indefinitely.

JOHN BIRDSALL is an ex-cook who writes about food. His essay in *Lucky Peach* #8, "America, Your Food Is So Gay," won a James Beard Award for food and culture writing. He lives in Oakland, California.

ANTHONY BOURDAIN is the Emmy-winning host of *Parts Unknown* on CNN.

MAREN CARUSO brings curiosity, an eye for light and beauty, and a love of collaboration to conceptual food and product still-life photography. Working out of a 2,000-square-foot daylight studio in San Francisco, Maren shoots for editorial and advertising clients including Wieden Kennedy, Draft FCB, Creature, Target, Levi's, Happy Baby, Kraft, Safeway, Williams-Sonoma, Phaidon, *Bon Appétit*, Chronicle Books, and Ten Speed Press, among others.

JULIA COOKE is the author of *The Other Side of Paradise: Life in the New Cuba*. She lives in New York, where she teaches at the New School.

MICHAEL DEFORGE draws comics in Toronto, Ontario. His short story collection, *A Body Beneath*, was published by Koyama Press in 2014, and his graphic novel, *First Year Healthy*, is being released by Drawn & Quarterly in 2015.

BUDI DHARMAWAN is an Indonesian independent photographer based in Yogyakarta, who is interested in social and cultural issues. He has contributed his work to Indonesian *National Geographic*, as well as *Le Monde* (FR), *Stern* (DE), and *Bulletin* (CH), among other publications. Budi doesn't really like to travel, but loves the fact that he keeps traveling anyway.

SAM D'ORAZIO has an adventurous spirit and will do anything for love. He is from Providence, Rhode Island. See his work at *samdorazio.com*.

LEE ELLIS's work has appeared in the *Believer* and on *newyorker.com*. Originally from northwest Florida, he currently lives in Paris.

SARAH ELTON is the author of three best-selling books about food, including *Consumed: Food for a Finite Planet* and for kids, *Starting from Scratch: What You Should Know about Food and Cooking*. She makes mithai for her family in Toronto.

ADAM LEITH GOLLNER is the author of *The Fruit Hunters* (Scribner) and *The Book of Immortality* (Scribner).

LISA HANAWALT lives in LA and her book, *My Dirty Dumb Eyes*, was published by Drawn & Quarterly in 2013. She's also the production designer of *BoJack Horseman*, now streaming on Netflix. Follow her work at *lisahanawalt.com*.

KENDYLL HILLEGAS is a Boston-based artist and illustrator. Her work focuses on capturing the emotional and narrative significance of food and everyday objects. She enjoys thrifting, pie baking, and binge-listening to audiobooks.

ELENI KALORKOTI is an illustrator of Scottish origin now living and working in lovely south London, where she can be found making pictures and eating fig rolls. Look for her on the Internet at *elenikalorkoti.com* and *@elenikalorkoti*.

MELATI KAYE is a freelance reporter based in Indonesia.

SCOTT KORB is the author, most recently, of *Light without Fire: The Making of America's First Muslim College* and co-editor of *Gesturing Toward Reality: David Foster Wallace and Philosophy*. He lives with his family in New York City.

MICHAEL LAISKONIS, formerly of Le Bernardin, is a pastry chef and Creative Director at the Institute of Culinary Education in New York City.

JESSICA LAMB-SHAPIRO is the author of *Promise Land: My Journey Through America's Self-Help Culture*. Her nonfiction and fiction have appeared in the *New York Times Magazine*, *Time.com*, *McSweeney's*, and the *Believer*.

CELINE LOUP is French born, East Coast raised. She earned her BFA in illustration from the Maryland Institute College of Art in 2010. Her aesthetics are informed by vintage lifestyle photography, Swedish electronic music, and French comic books. She is available for freelance work.

DAVIDE LUCIANO is a conceptual and fine art photographer and filmmaker based in NYC. He creates large-scale photographic prints that are cinematic in scope and compelling in content. Luciano's work has been exhibited in solo and group shows in Canada and the United States.

BRAD THOMAS PARSONS is the author of *Bitters: A Spirited History of a Classic Cure-All*. He is currently at work on a book about amaro to be published by Ten Speed Press.

LUCAS PETERSON lives and works in Los Angeles. Please send him love letters and secret driving shortcuts @lucaspeterson.

MONICA RAMOS is an illustrator, modern woman, and friend. View more work at *monramos.com*.

PAULA SEARING is an illustrator located in Brooklyn, New York. After growing up in upstate New York, she moved to the city to attend Parsons The New School for Design. Since then, she has exhibited internationally and had the pleasure of working with clients such as the *New York Times*, *Elle Décor*, and *BuzzFeed*.

MICHAEL SNYDER is a freelance food, travel, and design writer based (mostly) out of Mumbai, India. His writing has appeared in the *Washington Post*, the *New York Times*, *T Magazine*, and *Monocle*, among others. He also serves as a Contributing Editor for *Architectural Digest India*.

SCOTT TEPLIN sexualizes doughnut drawings in his spare time and professionally. NSFW: *teplin.com/donuts*.

WINNIE TRUONG is currently thinking about what she should grab for lunch in Toronto, Ontario, where she works full-time as an artist using pencil crayons to make little lines on paper. You can find her drawings at *winnietruong.com*.

MICHAEL TUNK takes photographs and magazines from the 1800s to the 1980s and re-contextualizes them into something beautiful. He takes refused detritus and spins a yarn of gold. He takes the weight from a hoarders home and fixes it into aesthetic candy. His pieces are never Photoshopped; he uses only X-acto blades and what's left of the bones in his wrists.

CARI VANDER YACHT is an illustrator living in Brooklyn, NY. She wrote this bio on her iPhone while holding a tiny pie.

ANDREA WAN is an artist and illustrator born in Hong Kong and raised in Vancouver, BC. She had a background in filmmaking before studying illustration and design in Denmark in 2008. Andrea is currently living and working in Berlin. Her work has been published and exhibited worldwide. *andreawan.com*

MIKE YING is a Masters of Architecture student at UCLA and buffalo wing–eating contest T-shirt winner.

THE PITCHFORK REVIEW

From your friends at Pitchfork comes a quarterly print publication of long-form feature stories, photography, design, cartoons, and other ephemera. *The Pitchfork Review* documents music culture—past and present.

IN THE LATEST ISSUE
David Bowie • Courtney Barnett • Robert Wyatt • El-P •
Sharon Van Etten • The Grateful Dead • NASA Nightclub •
Dory Previn • Phil Elverum • Photos • Comics • Recipes •
FREE 7" from Zola Jesus • A TON MORE!

THE BEST THING SINCE THIS SHIT

SPECIAL SUBSCRIPTION RATE FOR *LUCKY PEACH* READERS!

Enter "Lucky" at checkout for 15% off.
thepitchforkreview.com